MORE HAUNTED HOUSES

Also available in this series

Haunted Houses *Aidan Chambers*
Great British Ghosts *Aidan Chambers*
Great Sea Mysteries *Richard Garrett*
Hoaxes and Swindles *Richard Garrett*
True Tales of Detection *Richard Garrett*
Narrow Squeaks! *Richard Garrett*
Bushrangers Bold! *Frank Hatherley*
Scottish Ghosts *Sorche Nic Leodhas*
Airships and Balloons *Carey Miller*
Submarines! *Carey Miller*
The Boys' Book of the Sea *Nicholas Monsarrat*
Great Air Battles *Eric Williams*

Piccolo True Adventures

MORE HAUNTED HOUSES

Text illustrations by Chris Bradbury

Cover illustration by Brian Froude

Aidan Chambers

A Piccolo Original

Pan Books London and Sydney

First published 1973 by Pan Books Ltd,
Cavaye Place, London SW10 9PG
3rd printing 1975
ISBN 0 330 23470 6

Printed in Great Britain by
Cox & Wyman Ltd, London, Reading and Fakenham

For William Tucker

O'er all there hung the shadow of a fear;
A sense of mystery the spirit daunted;
And said, as plain as whisper in the ear,
The place is haunted!

– Thomas Hood

ACKNOWLEDGEMENT

The passages from *Ghosts I Have Seen* by Violet Tweedale are quoted by permission of Barrie and Jenkins Ltd.

CONTENTS

From the author

So many readers have written to me asking for more stories about haunted houses that I could not resist the temptation to write this second book. As I said in my introduction to the first collection,* I am not really very worried whether these stories are true or not; what I like about them, as I think most of those who wrote to me do too, is that they are all entertaining.

I'm not a ghost hunter, and I do not dabble in the occult; I've no stomach for that kind of thing, finding what seem to me to be better ways of spending my time. But, like most people, I'm puzzled by death and the big question it poses about an after-life. So perhaps I enjoy ghost stories not simply because they entertain me, but because at the same time, while I'm being amused by the ghostly fun, they help me turn over in my mind the far more serious and difficult problem of what becomes of the human spirit once the human body has ceased to function.

I cannot accept that the essential part of what we are – the part that makes us individual, unique beings – rots in the grave with our mortal flesh and bones. Ghost stories touch, albeit lightly, on that theme.

* *Haunted Houses* (Piccolo, 1971).

And if there are such 'things' as ghosts, why then we have grounds for believing that in one way or another, mysterious though it be, the human essence lives on beyond the grave.

The trouble with ghosts, of course, is that they seem to dislike scientific investigation and fade away into the walls as soon as anyone tries to subject them to it. So, in the end, belief in ghosts is always a matter of faith. And faith, though it is a powerful force in a man's life, can easily be misled and misplaced.

Which brings me full circle. I don't know whether the ghosts in this book ever actually haunted the houses they are supposed to have lived in. But I hope others will enjoy reading about them as much as I have enjoyed writing about them. I'm always pleased to get letters from readers who want to tell me what they thought, and to learn of ghosts they have come across or heard about. Anyone who wants to write to me can do so at this address: Aidan Chambers, c/o Pan Books Ltd, 33 Tothill Street, London SW1.

CHAPTER ONE

The ghost of Raynham Hall

About twenty miles from King's Lynn in Norfolk and five or so from the little town of Fakenham, there stands a magnificent seventeenth-century stately home, called Raynham Hall. It is the seat of the Marquesses of Townshend. The Townshends are a famous English family, but the ghost who haunts their home is perhaps more famous still. For nearly three hundred years the spectre of a lady dressed in brown has been seen in the house by all kinds of people from the humblest servant to a king of England. The eerie brown lady has been sketched and photographed and even shot at by a well-known author of books for children.

It all began with a strange young woman, Dorothy Walpole. Dorothy's father was a Member of Parliament and her brother, Sir Robert Walpole, became what we would now call Prime Minister – the first that ever was – in 1721. When Dorothy was a young girl her father (also called Robert) was made guardian of a thirteen-year-old viscount, Charles Townshend, a young nobleman who was himself later to be a great politician.

Charles Townshend and Dorothy Walpole liked each other at once, their liking grew into fondness

Raynham Hall

and finally, in their late teens, fondness turned into love. When Dorothy's father was asked by the two young people for permission to marry, he firmly forbade the match. There was nothing legally to prevent it; Charles was not Dorothy's brother, merely the ward of her father. But old Walpole was in a difficulty. What, he wondered, would people say if he allowed the marriage? Charles was a viscount and a rich one at that. Wouldn't people think that the marriage had been arranged simply so that the Walpoles could get their hands on the Townshend money and land? Old Walpole thought so, and no argument from his daughter or from Charles would change his mind. It just would not do, he said, for a family so much in the public eye as the Walpoles to lay themselves open to criticism, no matter how ill-founded in truth. The marriage was not to be.

Resigned to his fate, young Charles threw himself into his work and a year or two later married a daughter of Baron Pelham of Laughton.

Dorothy was not so easily settled and her disappointment rankled within her. Obey her father she must, and she had no power to prevent Charles from making the best of things and marrying someone else. Nor had she great public work to occupy her mind and salve the wound of her lost love. She did the only thing she could. She distracted herself with gay parties, entertainment, constant companionship among wealthy people who had little else to do but spend their money and their time with thoughtless abandon.

Eventually she turned up in Paris, and there, out of

her father's and brother's sight, she took up with some disreputable characters among whom was a not very gentlemanly gentleman, a rogue called Lord Wharton. Very soon, Dorothy was living with the rakish lord, and the pair of them were the talk of the town. Rumours circulated even in London about the life they lived together; but no one was foolish enough to let the Walpoles know what was being said about their relative.

Then, suddenly, in 1711 Charles Townshend's wife died. As soon as news of the event reached Dorothy she returned to Raynham. A year later she married Charles. She was twenty-six.

That might well have been that. Dorothy and Charles were blissfully happy; they were wealthy, important, powerful. Everything seemed set fair for the rest of their lives. But it was not to be. Those who are wealthy are envied, and those who are powerful make enemies. Charles had his share of both. What no one would tell the Walpoles, was now maliciously whispered to Charles Townshend. Did he know about his new wife's behaviour in Paris? Hadn't he heard of the affair with the rogue, Lord Wharton? To Charles the gossip was like a poison in his mind, a poison that contaminated his reason and killed his love for Dorothy. He was furious. He swore he'd have nothing more to do with his wife. Keep her he must, but he did not need to see or speak to her. Dorothy was confined to her rooms at Raynham Hall, was not allowed out, nor to have visitors.

Banished by her husband, the only man she had ever truly loved, secluded from her friends – so this unfortunate woman lived for another ten years or so, until, in 1726, she died. Some say it was a broken heart that killed her and it is easy to believe: she had had enough of sadness in her life, despite the advantages she began with. The records say she died of smallpox, and this too is easy to accept, for in those days smallpox was a common and deadly disease. But there is another more sinister story. According to this legend Dorothy died not from sadness or a common plague but from a broken neck, sustained when she stumbled down the grand oak staircase at the Hall – a tumble caused not by some accidental slip of the foot but by a deliberate push from behind.

Was Dorothy Townshend murdered? We shall never know now. But *if she was*, there would have been no trouble in having the nasty business hushed up. With a powerful father, a brother the first minister of the Government and a husband who knew royalty almost as well as his own family, it would have been easy enough to see that some common illness was stated on the death certificate as the cause of Dorothy's early and unhappy death.

Whatever the truth may be, Dorothy did not rest peacefully in her grave. Her spirit rose to walk the rooms and corridors where she had been confined, there to frighten her family, their servants and their guests through the years that followed. The accounts of her hauntings are numerous and often well documented; of these I have selected a few to retell here because of their particular interest.

In 1786 the Townshends were made marquesses and Raynham Hall became a meeting place for the most notable people in the land. On one occasion King George the Fourth – that dashing, devil-may-care George who as Prince Regent had been the sometimes-scandalized talk of Europe – came to stay. Very little frightened him. But Dorothy's ghost certainly did. His Majesty of England woke in the dead of night to behold at his bedside the figure of a lady dressed in brown and with, the king later said, 'dishevelled hair and a face of ashy paleness'. That His Majesty discovered a woman in his bedroom was by no means an unusual event – though usually he had invited them there beforehand. It was normally something that gave him great pleasure. But not this time. He took one brief look at the brown lady and fled the room, garbed only in the royal nightgown and night cap. Round the house he stormed, rousing all and sundry, trembling in fear and shouting in imperial wrath. When the company had assembled, tousled, in dishabille, but curious, the king regaled them with his startling encounter and concluded by swearing, 'I will not pass another hour in this accursed house, for tonight I have seen that which I hope to God I may never see again.'

If ghosts have a sense of humour, Dorothy's must have laughed; and if it was revenge she looked for, then she had some small satisfaction. No one who wished to remain at the centre of national life in the days of gay George offended the king. And George was clearly out of sorts after his experience at the Hall. Perhaps that is why gamekeepers were ordered to stand nightly watch, along with some of Townshend's friends, to see whether the king had really been attended in his room by a ghost or whether – as most people insisted on believing – some jackanapes had simply played a trick on his royal sire.

At any rate, for two nights men kept silent guard in and outside the house but never a sight or sound other than the night birds and the natural creakings of an old house disturbed their watch. On the third night, however, Dorothy appeared, walking down a corridor. Gamekeepers and gentlemen stood riveted to the spot, terrified. Except one. He must have possessed a tougher nerve than the others. He walked boldly towards the spectre and stood firmly in its path. But without pause or sign of disturbance at the fact that somebody obstructed its path, Dorothy's ghost walked on, reached the brave fellow, and passed right through him before disappearing into a wall at the end of the passage.

The bold gentleman was shaken to his boots and stared in wonder after the apparition. As well he might; it is not every day you stand four-square on your sober feet and watch a 'something' pass right *through* your body! He had felt, the poor chap said, as if an icy cloud of smoke had passed into his bones and out again.

In 1835 the brown lady chose Christmas for an elaborate haunting that had interesting repercussions. Raynham Hall was full of guests making merry – too merry for Dorothy's taste, perhaps. Late one night two guests, Colonel Loftus and a man named Hawkins, saw the ghost standing outside the then Lady Townshend's bedroom. Colonel Loftus was the Lady's brother, so it is not surprising that he was alarmed to discover a ghost hovering about outside his sister's room.

With commendable military aplomb, Loftus ran at the ghost, which floated off down the passage, the colonel in hot pursuit. But even a soldier, gallant though he be, is no match for a determined apparition and soon Loftus found himself chasing alone down dark, deserted corridors. The brown lady had vanished.

She was, however, back again next night. And once again it was Loftus who came face to face with her, this time on the grand staircase – a favourite place for the brown lady's haunts and down which, it will be remembered, the living Dorothy had fallen to her early death. Later the colonel described what he saw: a stately woman dressed in rich brown brocade and a coif – a cap-like head-dress that covered the back and sides of the head. All this was unremarkable, hardly cause for much fear and astonishment. What startled the colonel, as it had done others before him and would do others afterwards, was that, as he said, 'although her features were clearly defined, where her eyes should have been were nothing but dark hollows'.

A ghost with all the features of a human being – except the eyes! Every account speaks of those ghastly empty sockets in the skull. From them seemed to flow the feeling of evil malice that everyone who beheld the spectacle remarked on. And, strangely enough, those blind eye-holes appeared elsewhere. For many years until it was sold in 1904 at Christie's, the famous London auctioneers, there hung at Raynham a painting of Dorothy Walpole. In daylight, the portrait was ordinary enough; it depicted an eighteenth-century lady with big, bright eyes, dressed in brown brocade with yellow trimmings and a ruff round her neck. But in candle light the whole picture changed. The face in that soft illumination took on an evil stare. And when the light was shone from certain angles the flesh seemed to shrink from the face, those beautiful, large eyes seemed to fade away, until the head was left like a skull bare of all but the shining bone.

Knowing of the eerie portrait, it is not to be wondered at that a seasoned soldier like Colonel Loftus was scared to his marrow by his meeting that festive season with the spirit of the same Lady Dorothy whose picture hung in the Hall. Nor had the ghost finished its work for that night, as a guest learned next morning when, after hearing the shattered colonel's tale, he asked the master of the house, Lord Townshend, whether he believed the Hall was indeed haunted by a ghost. 'I am forced to believe it,' Lord Townshend told him, 'for she ushered me to my room last night.'

Christmas merrymaking soon died that year at Raynham, strangled like early spring blossom by a chill night frost. First the colonel, then Lord Townshend, and after that a succession of guests were sobered by a sudden encounter with the eyeless, malevolent appearance before them of the brown lady, until at last the party broke up and the visitors returned to the less harrowing comfort of their own homes.

'Once again it was Loftus who came face to face with her, this time on the grand staircase . . .'

It is at this point that the famous author I mentioned at the beginning of this curious story comes on the scene. His name was Captain Frederick Marryat, who after many years at sea had written stories for boys that are read and enjoyed still: *Mr Midshipman Easy* and *The Children of the New Forest** among others. He had come to settle at Langham Manor, very near Raynham Hall. Marryat did not believe in ghosts, and unlike many seamen was not in the least superstitious. It was his opinion, when he heard of the brown lady's antics that Christmas, that someone was playing tricks. He offered the theory that smugglers, who were plentiful in those parts of Norfolk, were using some ruined buildings near the Hall for hiding places, and that they were pretending to be ghosts in order to divert the Townshends' attention from the illegal traffic going on under their noses. This was not such an unlikely possibility as it may now seem. Smugglers have been known in the past to play the ghost as a way of frightening off unwanted intruders.

Lord Townshend, at any rate, took Marryat seriously, and invited the author to stay in order to try and prove his theory. Marryat took up the challenge. He insisted first of all on being given the haunted bedroom to sleep in – the same room, in fact, where the portrait of Dorothy hung.

For some time nothing untoward occurred. Then one night, after talking till late with Lord Townshend's two young nephews, Marryat went to his room and began to undress in preparation for bed.

* Available in Pan Books.

He had stripped to his vest and trousers when the young men knocked at his door and insisted the Captain put an end to an argument that had broken out between them about a certain gun. Marryat agreed to go to the room of one of the young men and adjudicate the disagreement. As he left his own room he grabbed up a loaded pistol he kept ready at his bedside and laughingly said, 'In case we meet the brown lady!'

The dispute was soon settled, and Marryat's young friends, joining in the joke, insisted on escorting him back along the corridor, 'In case you are kidnapped by the ghost!'

The joke soon turned sour.

The passage between the two rooms was a long one, and as it was late at night the servants had already put out the lights. As the three men walked down the passage they were surprised to see a woman carrying a lamp approaching them. They were surprised, not because they thought the woman was the ghost, but because this particular corridor and the rooms leading off it were reserved for the bachelor guests staying at the Hall; women were not expected to go there. But here was a woman, bold as could be, walking towards them, and here too was the famous seaman-author dressed in nothing more than his vest and pants: a sight not thought fit in those days for a gentlewoman's sensitive gaze! There was only one thing to do and the three men did it: they pushed open the nearest door and hustled inside, intending to wait politely until the straying lady had passed by before going on their way.

The lady did not go modestly by, however; instead she stopped at the doorway and looked unblinking at the embarrassed men. As they looked back at her, their embarrassment turned to panic-stricken fear. Each man knew at once who it was in the corridor. She resembled exactly the portrait hanging in the haunted bedroom. And on this occasion the eyes were plainly visible: large, bright, staring. Dumb-struck, Marryat and his two companions watched, unmoving; and all three saw that it was directly into Marryat's eyes that the ghost was looking. Then across the ghostly face a wide and wicked grin slowly spread.

That diabolical smile so frightened Marryat that without pausing for a moment's thought he stepped forward and fired one shot from his pistol. The bullet passed unhindered through the ghostly form and went on to slice its way through the door opposite. At that, the grinning brown lady slowly vanished.

The sceptical Marryat doubted no more. Shocked out of his wits by the incident, he could later find no other explanation for his experience but to acknowledge that what he had seen and fired his pistol at had indeed been something unnatural, something that conformed to none of the known laws of life. He left the Hall quite convinced that whatever caused the brown lady's appearances, it was not the ingenuity of clever smugglers.

Little more is heard of the brown lady for many years – maybe Marryat's pot shot had been enough even for a ghost to endure! – but in November 1926 she was met once again on the oak staircase by the

Marquess of Townshend – who was, at the time, only a boy – and a young friend of his. Not surprisingly, they were scared stiff and somehow the newspapers got wind of the renewed activity of the Raynham spook. The marquess and his friend were carefully questioned. Neither of them had heard the family legend, and the portrait, it will be remembered, had been sold in 1904, years before the boys had been born. Yet the descriptions each lad gave of the figure they had met on the stairs fitted exactly the usual appearance of the eyeless, evil-faced brown lady.

The final climactic event in this long saga of persistent psychical phenomena brings us to the afternoon of September 19th, 1936. On that day a professional photographer, Mr Indre Shira, assisted by a Mr Provand, was busily taking pictures of various parts of Raynham Hall at the request of Lady Townshend. In the afternoon they came to the oak staircase and set up the camera and flash gear in preparation for photographing this fine feature of the house. Mr Provand had taken one exposure and was putting a new plate into the camera when Mr Shira saw a vapoury form taking shape on the stairs. Quite taken aback, the photographer was astonished to see the form gradually gather itself into what he thought looked like a woman dressed in a flowing, transparent gown, rather like a wedding dress. Once formed, the vision began to float slowly down the stairs towards the two men.

Mr Provand, busy with the camera, had seen none of this. Mr Shira excitedly shouted to his companion to expose the plate quickly, and pointed frantically at the ghost coming steadily on down the stairs. Luckily, Mr Provand reacted instinctively and did as he was told. The flash went off; and with that the ghost seems to have vanished.

The picture taken, Mr Provand, still unaware of why his partner should be so excited, asked what was going on. A ghost had been coming down the stairs, Mr Shira told him. Nonsense, Mr Provand replied. Someone was playing tricks, or the flash had caused an optical illusion. Shira was seeing things that weren't there. But Mr Shira was not to be put off so easily. He bet Mr Provand five pounds that when the plate was developed a ghost would show on the picture.

Mr Shira won his bet. When the camera plate was processed sure enough a cloudy form, resembling precisely the form he had described, showed on the photograph. On December 16th, 1936, the picture was printed in a magazine called *Country Life*. Now a number of photographs have been published from time to time which purport to show ghosts. But faking such evidence is all too easy. Many experts were therefore consulted about Mr Shira's snapshot of the spectre on the Raynham Hall staircase, and many of them decided that whatever it is that appears on the exposed plate it is certainly not the result of fakery.

One thing is fascinating about that lucky incident. In all the recorded appearances, Lady Dorothy's unhappy spirit is always dressed in brown brocade with a ruff at its neck and a coif on its head. But in Mr Shira's photograph it presents itself as a figure dressed, as far as one can see, in a flowing veil and a diaphanous gown. Is it the brown lady that Mr Shira's camera caught that September afternoon? And if it is, did that sad spirit manifest itself especially for the occasion in Dorothy's wedding clothes on the very stairs where by ill-fortune or murderous design she may well have fallen to her death? No one can blame that spirit if it did; for Lady Dorothy's wedding day must have been one of the few happy days in her short, unhappy adult life – the day she at last married the man she had loved since childhood and who was soon to turn so cruelly against her, shutting her up in a few lonely rooms in that large and beautiful house.

CHAPTER TWO

Death at Breckles Hall

If you visit the Elizabethan manor Breckles Hall, in Norfolk, do not go at midnight, for at midnight it is just possible that you might see a ghostly sight so terrible, so frightful, that men have died from looking on it. Men like Jim Mace, poacher, drunkard, boaster.

One Christmas time in the early years of this century, bombastic Jim was boozing with his pals in the local public house near Breckles Hall. It was late at night; outside crisp snow glistened in the steely light of a sharp-edged moon. In the hedges and trees fat partridges, bred by the local gentry as fodder for their guns and their tables, roosted silent and safe. And in the dark of his cottage the deaf old gamekeeper lay snoring in his bed.

As the merry night wore on, Jimmy and his cronies drank themselves silly. And their conversation grew as silly as they looked. They joked, and thought themselves mighty wits, though what they said, whether it had humour or not, no one sober could have told, for their speech by now was slurred beyond recognition. But all the party roared at every slobbered word, and each man thumped the beer-soaked table and cheered and stamped his feet. And

Breckles Hall

between jokes they argued the toss, and boasted of their prowess as poacher or fighter, tale-teller or wag, and each man thought himself just that much grander than the next.

Until suddenly a poaching pal of Jimmy's, the biggest swollen head of them all, upped to his feet and said:

'Jimmy and me,' he burbled, 'Jimmy and me is goin' ter have a brace o' them fat partridge birds for Christmas. We'll take our guns an' shoot them down and that old 'keeper, why, he's too deaf ter hear.'

'Now just you listen ter me, my boy,' said an old chap who had been sitting nearby, 'you just remember the coach an' four.'

For a blank-faced moment, Jimmy's pal stared at the old man, first to focus his eyes upon the old fellow, and then to make sense of the words in his drink-soaked brain.

Everybody knew about the ghostly coach and four that was said to come galloping down the Breckles Hall road at midnight now and then, when the Hall was left unoccupied. Silently it came, speeding along till it stopped at the Hall door. And as it came, every window in the empty house lit up brightly, and inside, if you dared to look, which few had done, you saw a ball in full swing, the dancers swirling round the room with gay abandon, though never a sound from mouth or gadding foot was heard. The coach would stop, footmen climb down, the coach door open. Then out would step a grand and beautiful lady. And it was she, men said, that you must avoid, for she would look a man in the eyes and he'd drop dead where he stood.

The sozzled poacher knew the story, like everyone else in the bar that night. But the beer had made him proud and fearless and full of hot courage.

' 'Tis nowt,' he said, scorning the old chap's words.

'The Hall's empty tonight,' the old man mused quietly.

But Jimmy's pal wasn't to be put off. With a nod, he pushed his way out of the pub, Jimmy close behind.

'We shall shoot them ghosties an' all!' he said as he left, and laughed.

So Jimmy and his mate set off, full of dutch courage. They called at Jimmy's cottage and picked up a gun and a bag, and off they went into the nipping frost, searching the hedges for game.

Drunk they might have been, but their shots found a mark or two and before long their bag was bulging and their craving satisfied. Till Jimmy remembered the empty Hall.

'Let's us two go an' rouse them boggarts,' he said and his pal readily agreed; so off they went towards the house.

When they reached the mansion, the place was quiet as the grave and black as the fire back. It towered up over them, deep shadows where the windows were, like jet-black eyes, and the snow-covered roof like a white wig.

Jimmy stumbled up to a window pane and tried to peer into the inner darkness.

'Don't see no bogies,' he said, and he sounded almost disappointed. 'Try the door, boy.' And he felt his way along the wall until he found the front door, a huge affair, and he rattled it against its locks.

No sooner had he done so than the village church clock chimed out twelve strokes as clear as crystal, ringing on the freezing air of the still night.

And as the last stroke sounded, round the corner of the Hall drive swept a coach and four. Its horses stepped high, but their pounding hooves struck no noise from the ground. Its lamps shone like yellow stars; its two footmen behind and the driver in front sat stiff and still as tailor's dummies, their unblinking eyes glancing neither right nor left.

Instantly, every window in the house lit up, ablaze with light, and the great front door, which Jimmy only a moment before had shaken against its locks, swung wide open.

Cramped to the spot by fear and astonishment, the two men watched as the coach came closer and drew in by the door no more than a couple of feet from where they watched. Down the footmen climbed, just as everyone said they did, opened the carriage door, unfolded the steps and then stood back one to either side.

A second's dreadful pause. Then from the coach, gracefully as only a woman can, came the most dazzlingly lovely lady the poor stricken poachers had ever seen in their simple lives. Her jewels winked from neck and arms and hands; her dress, flimsy as dawn mist, billowed about her. Down the carriage steps she came, reached the ground, and raised her head.

She looked straight into the transfixed eyes of poor Jimmy.

For a while the world seemed to have stopped turning through space, and time to have lost all meaning. Then slowly Jimmy Mace opened his mouth and let

'Cramped to the spot by fear and astonishment, the two men watched as the coach came closer . . .'

out a long, stark, piercing howl that sliced to the nerve of the silent winter night.

That anguished cry brought Jimmy's pal to his senses, sobered him in a trice, and sent him running madly off towards the village as if all the devils in hell were at his twinkling heels. When he reached the houses he ran from one to the next, calling frantically for help. But as soon as he told his tale not a man would return with him to the Hall.

Next morning, however, the parson and some of the villagers did go there. Not a sign of the coach could they find, not a hoof print in the soft snow, not a wheel-track anywhere. But lying in front of the locked main door of the magnificent old house was Jimmy Mace's body, dead, frozen, and with such a look of dread etched upon his face that few men present could bear the sight. The mysterious, beautiful, ghostly lady of Breckles Hall had claimed another victim.

CHAPTER THREE

Some London ghosts

London has more than its fair share of haunted buildings. Most well-known places, from the Tower itself to Westminster Cathedral and the Bank of England, boast a ghost or two. The most famous – and gruesome – story of all is about the unearthly horror that for many years during the last century caused 50 Berkeley Square to stand unoccupied on its expensive Mayfair site because no one had the courage to face the vile 'thing' that lived on the second floor.* But there are many other London ghosts, quite as interesting if not so fatal for those who see them.

Ghosts can be tantalizing, appearing and disappearing without a word of explanation, leaving behind shocked and puzzled mortals, who, by some inexplicable accident, chanced to catch a glimpse of them as they passed by. For this reason many ghost stories are short, being little more than brief accounts of a moment in someone's life when the laws of normal existence were suspended and the unknown invaded the known, taking everyone by surprise. Rather than dress up some of London's more entertaining spectres in the kind of detail that might give

* The story is told in the companion to this volume, *Haunted Houses* by Aidan Chambers (Piccolo).

them spine-chilling, but nevertheless completely spurious attractions, I have collected a few together in all their stark brevity. They can speak for themselves, or, rather, the few facts known about their appearances can speak for them.

The ghost in the London Museum

Some years ago, a workman helping to dig the foundations for a warehouse being built near St Paul's Cathedral unearthed an old wooden box which was found to contain a horde of jewels: gold necklaces, rings, and other ornaments – about a hundred and fifty pieces in all. This lucky strike was taken to the house of an expert who worked at the London Museum in order to get his opinion as to the real value and age of the items. The expert told the government about the find (as by law he had to do) and kept the jewels in his house for a couple of weeks so that he could study them in peace.

The precious ornaments had been in the house only a few hours when odd things began to happen. It was a hot June day; the horde was delivered at about six o'clock in the evening. At about ten that night, the expert and his daughter were sitting in the room where the jewels had been placed when suddenly they both began shivering as though they were cold. Naturally, both of them were puzzled; the night was warm and sticky and there seemed to be no reason why they should each begin to shiver at that moment. They did not associate the shivering with the newly arrived treasure; but if they made no such connexion that first night, they did very soon after when a friend called the next day.

The expert's friend was interested in psychic phenomena – in everything to do with the supernatural and the occult. Nevertheless, the expert and his daughter were taken aback when, as they were showing their visitor the jewels, he said that he could see a tall, thin man dressed in Elizabethan costume standing by the table onwhich the jewels were spread. Furthermore, he said, the Elizabethan gentleman was angry; the jewels had belonged to him and he wanted to know who had allowed them to be moved from their hiding place.

Now the ghost and what it had to say could be seen and heard only by the visitor, and it is quite possible that he was making the whole thing up. But this was by no means the end of the matter. When the museum expert had studied the jewels to his satisfaction, they were taken to the London Museum where they were to stay permanently. Two or three years later, the expert was visited by a professional medium (a person who claims to have special powers which allow him to see and contact ghostly spirits). The medium knew nothing of the jewels or of the story of the angry Elizabethan gentleman who claimed to be their owner. Yet when they went into the room in the expert's house where the jewels had been kept two years or so before, the medium announced – to everyone's consternation – that he could see a figure standing near his host's daughter. The medium described the ghost – and every detail agreed with the description given by the expert's friend. Furthermore, the medium said, the ghost disliked the girl so much he feared that it might attempt to harm her! The only reason anybody could think of for the ghost's ill-feeling was that the girl had helped her father to clean and polish the jewels.

Only one clue has so far come to light that might help explain this strange story. One day a woman who was looking at the ornaments on show at the museum fell down in a faint. When she was revived, she said she had seen blood on a gold necklace and that she felt sure the woman who had once worn it had been murdered. The necklace was closely inspected; there was no trace of blood on it. What the woman had seen must have been ghostly blood!

Who was the angry Elizabethan who was visible only to those with psychic powers? The murdered woman's husband, perhaps – or her murderer? Had he buried the priceless jewels after stealing them and died himself before he could recover and dispose of them? We probably shall never know – which is just what I mean about ghosts being tantalizing creatures!

The ghostly monks of St Dunstan's Church, East Acton

Many churches claim to be haunted by monks; St Dunstan's is one of them and one of the most interesting and best documented.

During the Middle Ages a monastery certainly stood where St Dunstan's now is, so perhaps it is not surprising that on many occasions people have seen ghostly figures walking up the main aisle of the church. One vicar, the Reverend Anton-Stevens, who began his work in the church in 1944 and died in 1966, frequently witnessed monks in golden-brown habits, their hoods raised over their heads, walking towards the altar. He even talked to one of the monks, who, the vicar claimed, dictated an article on Confirmation which he, the vicar, published in the parish magazine.

Among other people who said they had seen the monks was a churchwarden. He also heard them play the organ, and told Mr Kenneth Mason, a reporter from the *Daily Graphic*.

Mr Mason had heard about the haunting and wanted to try and prove or disprove it, one way or another. So he spent a November evening in the building. For a while nothing unusual happened, and Mr Mason grew so tired he fell asleep. After a time, he suddenly woke up and at once saw walking towards him down the aisle six grey-clad and hooded monks. Mason got up from his seat and stood right in the path of the procession. The ghosts did not stop nor did they disappear. Instead they walked right through the astonished reporter!

Mason was certain that what he had witnessed was a ghostly manifestation and not a figment of his imagination. Whether he did see six monastic ghosts or not, the St Dunstan's haunting is one of those which have been testified to by so many people that, if you are at all inclined to believe in ghosts, you find it difficult to dismiss too lightly.

The Bank of England's ghost

The Bank of England has a nickname, The Old Lady of Threadneedle Street, and some people think that the nickname comes from the Bank's sad old ghost!

It happened that in 1811 a former employee of the Bank, a man called Philip Whitehead, was caught forging cheques. He was arrested, tried at the Old Bailey, and sentenced to death. To Whitehead's sister, Sarah, her brother's execution was such a heavy blow that she suffered for the rest of her life from mental illness. In those days she would have been called mad.

Every day after the hanging of her brother she would arrive at the Bank and wait forlornly for him to come out from work, as once, in better days, he used to do. That lonely, bereaved figure became very familiar in Threadneedle Street – the Old Lady, ever sorrowing, ever waiting for a brother she must have dearly loved but would never see again.

Many years went by; then at last, Sarah died. Out of pity for her, she was buried in the old churchyard that used to belong to the Bank and which has since been turned into a garden. There, it's said, her ghost has been seen from time to time, waiting still, no doubt, for her unfortunate brother to come and join her.

The Tower of London

The Tower is the most haunted place in this much

haunted city, and, considering all that has happened there down the years, that should surprise no one.

In *Haunted Houses*, I have written about Anne Boleyn's frequent startling appearances, sometimes wearing her head, sometimes without! But another of Henry the Eighth's many victims is said to make even more dramatic entrances back into this world on the anniversary of her death on the executioner's block. This is the Countess of Salisbury, daughter of the Duke of Clarence. She did not die willingly – few of Henry's victims did – nor did she die easily. Even in those days, when people gathered to watch executions in the same way as people these days go to watch football matches, the onlookers found the Countess' death a messy and sickening experience. So it is still when her ghost's head falls from her ghostly body in a re-enactment of that disgusting scene.

The ghost is observed, and heard too, as it runs from an equally ghostly executioner, screaming in fear and panic-stricken terror, until at last it is caught, as the real-life Countess was, and has its head hacked off by a rain of blows from the spectral executioner's inexpertly wielded axe.

Less gruesome but more fascinating is the story told by Edward Swifte, Keeper of the Crown Jewels in 1817. He and his family lived in the Tower in accommodation that went with the job. One Saturday night in October, Mr Swifte was having supper in Martin Tower with his wife, her sister and his young son. All the doors and windows were shut, for the night was unpleasant, and Mrs Swifte was about to

The Countess of Salisbury

take a drink when she stopped, the glass halfway to her lips, and said, 'Dear God! What is that?'

Her husband at once looked up, following the direction of his wife's staring eyes. He saw what he later described as 'a cylindrical figure, like a glass tube' floating suspended in the air between the table and the ceiling. The thing was as thick as a man's arm and seemed to be filled with liquid, part white, part blue, that swirled about inside.

For two minutes or so the tube hung before the amazed eyes of Edward and his wife. Edward's young son and Mrs Swifte's sister could see nothing unusual and sat watching the other two, thinking they had gone mad.

After hovering above the table, the object began to move round it, quite slowly and smoothly, until it came to a stop over Mrs Swifte's right shoulder.

This was too much for the poor woman. She screamed, and collapsed over the table, her hands grasped round her head to shield it. 'Lord, it has seized me!' she yelled out.

His wife's distress drove Swifte into action. Taking up a chair, he crashed it against the floating cylinder, which vanished from sight at the very moment of impact.

No one has ever explained convincingly what it was Swifte and his wife saw. All we do know is that a few days afterwards a sentry saw something materialize from under the door leading into the Jewel Room, something which, he said, formed itself into the likeness of a huge bear. The sentry stabbed at it with his bayonet, but hit nothing except the wooden door, at which he fainted from shock. He was found and brought back to his senses, but died a few days later.

One of the saddest tales about the Tower's ghosts concerns the two boy princes smothered, it is believed, on the orders of their uncle, the Duke of Gloucester, so that he could seize the crown and become King Richard the Third. Prince Edward was thirteen when he died, proclaimed king but never throned. His younger brother, Richard, was Duke of York. Their bodies were buried first in the floor of Wakefield Tower, but were later dug up and re-interred at the bottom of the staircase leading from White Tower to St John's Chapel. Many times since their ghosts have been seen walking hand in hand through the rooms where during their short lives they were imprisoned and finally murdered.

The bird-ghost of Lincoln's Inn

Proving beyond doubt that a ghost *is* a ghost – and not a trick of the light or a fantasy of the mind – and that a house is really haunted – and not simply disturbed by natural causes hard to discover – is an almost impossibly difficult task. People can deceive themselves very easily, and superstition is still a strong force in many people's lives: they still throw salt over their shoulders after they have spilt some, avoid walking under ladders, and carry lucky charms to ward off unknown evil. And many boys and girls have lain shivering in bed, frightened out of their senses, the bedclothes pulled over their heads, because they think they have seen a ghost when all that happened was that a loose floorboard creaked in the stillness of the night and the moon shone suddenly from behind a cloud and cast an eerie light on the curtains.

There are unscrupulous people, out for money or fame or simply for a cheap thrill at other people's expense, who have been known to manufacture tricks by which to deceive the unwary into thinking their houses are haunted. And ghost hunters, people with a genuine scientific interest in the supernatural, go to great lengths to make their investigations of reported hauntings as foolproof as possible. But even so the results of their inquiries are rarely, if ever, conclusive. They are, however, often very interesting.

Here, in the words of the investigators themselves, is an account of a ghost investigation that took place on the night of Saturday, May 11th to Sunday, May 12th, 1901 in a house in Lincoln's Inn, London. The two men involved were the *Daily Mail*'s news editor, Mr Ralph D. Blumenfeld, and the editor of *Cassell's Magazine*, Mr Max Pemberton. Both these men were experienced reporters, used to sorting out fact from fiction, so their account can be trusted. Mr Blumenfeld, who wrote the story, did not believe or disbelieve in ghosts – he was merely curious to try and find out the truth.

The house where the investigation took place was an old one, full of lawyers' offices. Four rooms were occupied by a writer friend of Mr Blumenfeld's who said that 'things happened' at night. Many other people had lived in the flat, but all of them, except Mr Blumenfeld's friend, had left hurriedly after a short stay. Finally, Mr Blumenfeld's friend left too, saying he could stand it no longer. But he would not say what it was he couldn't bear to live with! So the two newsmen decided to find out for themselves what it was that caused such an upset in the lives of those who inhabited the apartment.

This is how the account, published in the *Daily Mail* on Thursday, May 16th, 1901, continues with the story:

> I arranged an all-night sitting in these rooms where 'things happened'. Two chairs and a table were absolutely the only furniture left in the place. We unlocked the front door a little before midnight on Saturday last, locked it behind us, and turned on the electric light. We were alone in the house.
>
> After mounting the stairs from the outer door, there was a smallish room through which we passed into the principal apartment. This had a fireplace on the north wall and two doors in the south wall, through one of which was the entrance from the stairs. The other door was that of another small room which had no means of communication, so that there was no connexion between the two small rooms save through the large room.
>
> We searched the place thoroughly, closed and locked the windows, and pulled down the registers of the three fireplaces. There was absolutely no possibility of anyone being hidden anywhere in the rooms. There were no cupboards, no recesses, no dark corners and no sliding panels. Even a black beetle could not have escaped unnoticed.
>
> The walls were entirely naked, there were no blinds or curtains. On the floor of the two smaller rooms we spread powdered chalk, such as is used for polishing dancing floors. This was to trace anybody or anything that might come or go.

We had been warned that nothing happened in a room in which folks were watching. The doors leading to the little rooms were closed, and we sat in the big room and waited. We were both very wide awake, entirely calm, self-possessed and sober, expectant and receptive, and in no way excited or nervous. It was then about a quarter past midnight.

We talked in ordinary terms, told each other tales, exchanged experiences, for we had both travelled a good deal; and curiously enough discovered we had a mutual friend whom we had never mentioned before, although we had known each other for years. I only mention these trivialities in order to imply that so far as I am able to judge we were in quite an ordinary frame of mind. We did not deem it necessary to feel each other's pulses or take one another's temperatures, but I am convinced that having done so much we should have found ourselves to be entirely normal.

At seventeen minutes to one, the door opposite to us on the right leading to the little room to which there was no communication save through the room in which we were sitting, unlatched itself and opened slowly to its full width. The electric light was on in all the rooms. The click of the turning of the door handle was very audible. We waited expectantly. Nothing happened.

At four minutes to one precisely, the same thing occurred to the door on the left. Both doors were now standing wide open. We had been silent for a few seconds, watching the doors. Then we spoke

'This is unusual,' said I.

'Yes,' said the other man. 'Let's see if there's any resistance.'

We both rose, crossed the room and, expecting something, found nothing. The doors closed in the usual way, without opposition or resistance.

'Draught, of course,' was our comment, and we sat down again. But we knew there was no possibility of draught, because everything was tight shut. While the two doors had stood open we had both noticed that there was no mark on the sprinkled chalk.

We talked again, but there was a tension, a restraint, which we had not felt before, I cannot explain it, but it was there. Longish silences ensued, and I am sure we were both wide awake.

At 1.32 – my watch was on the table with a pencil and a slip of paper on which I noted the times – the right-hand door opened again, exactly as before. The latch clicked, the brass handle turned and slowly the door swung back to its full width. There was no jar or recoil when it became fully open. The opening process lasted about eleven seconds. At 1.37 the left-hand door opened as before, and both doors stood wide. We did not rise, but looked on and waited.

At 1.40 both doors closed simultaneously of their own accord, swinging slowly and gently to within about eight inches of the lock, when they slammed with a slight jar; and both latches clicked loudly, the one a fraction of a second later than the other. Between 1.45 and 1.55 this happened twice again, but the opening and closing were in no case simultaneous. There were thus four unaided openings and closings. (The first time we had closed them ourselves.)

The last openings took place at 2.7 and 2.9 and we both noticed marks on the chalk in the two little rooms. We sprang up and went to the doorways.

The marks were clearly defined bird's footprints in the middle of the floor, three in the left-hand room and five in the right-hand room. The marks were identical, and exactly 2 inches in size. We are neither of us ornithologists, but we compared them to the footprints of a bird about the size of a turkey. There were three toes and a short spur behind. The footprints converged diagonally towards the doors of the big room, and each one was clearly and sharply defined, with no blurring of outline or drag of any sort.

This broke up our sitting. We raised our voices to normal pitch, measured the footprints and made a sketch of them, lighted our pipes and sat down in the big room. Nothing more happened: the doors remained open, and the footprints clearly visible. It was just half past two.

We waited till half past three, discussing things we knew nothing about. Then we went home, locking the outer door behind us and dropping the key in an envelope into the letter-box of the house agent's office nearby. On the Embankment we were greeted by an exquisite opal and mother-of-pearl sunrise.

I have stated here exactly what happened, in a

bald matter-of-fact narrative. I explain nothing, I understand nothing. I am not convinced nor converted nor contentious. I have simply recorded facts. And the curious thing about it is that my curiosity has not been cured.

Like so many such accounts, this strange and macabre tale has been argued about publicly and privately ever since that news story appeared in the *Daily Mail*, but no one has ever successfully explained how bird's footprints got into the chalk of those two apartment rooms, nor whether it might have been a ghostly bird that imprinted them. But perhaps this is why so many people like ghost stories: because they linger in the mind long after they are first heard or read, puzzling, and – yes – haunting us as we search for an answer to the problems they pose.

CHAPTER FOUR

The ghost who saved a life

The two-hundred-year-old house, Elm Vicarage near Wisbech in Cambridgeshire, is said to be haunted by a curly haired monk called Ignatius, who saved the life of the rector's wife.

The story began not many years ago with the thud of footsteps heard one night in an upstairs room. The first time it happened, the then rector, the Reverend Bradshaw, went at once to find out who was poking about his home uninvited. But he found no one. A number of times more the footsteps sounded, always at night. And each time the rector tried to discover the cause. Despite careful searches not a living soul, nor any possible explanation for the noise was found anywhere.

Then one day just at dusk in an upstairs corridor Mrs Bradshaw solved the mystery. The footsteps were the noise not of any living person, but of a ghost. At first all Mrs Bradshaw could see in the gloomy light was a thin shape outlined – like the outline of a drawing – on the air. But slowly, as she watched, the outline filled in until at last she could see that the figure was a man aged about thirty, with dark curly hair, thin features, and clothes that looked like a monk's brown habit and sandals.

He can have been no ordinary ghost, this ethereal monk, and Mrs Bradshaw can have been no ordinary woman, for as the figure materialized he kept on walking towards Mrs Bradshaw who, in turn, went on walking towards the ghost. As they passed each other in the narrow corridor, they brushed together. At that moment, as though there was nothing at all unusual in the meeting, the monk murmured, 'Do be careful.'

At that most people would have fled the scene, or fainted, or just stood there and screamed. Not Mrs Bradshaw – courageous woman. She at once replied by asking the ghost who he thought he was.

'Ignatius,' the monk said unperturbed, 'the bell ringer.'

Then he disappeared.

Only after this brief but extraordinary encounter did Mrs Bradshaw begin to hear the church bell tolling the mournful, rhythmic tone of the death-knell. There would have been little surprising in this, had she not heard it in the middle of the night when funerals are not generally held, and when she and her husband and the rest of the village lay safely in their beds. On the first occasion this happened, Mrs Bradshaw mentioned it to her husband next morning and was somewhat surprised to learn that he had heard nothing at all and had slept peacefully throughout the night. Nor could the puzzled rector's wife find anyone else who had heard what to her had been a very distinct sound. But later that same day a death did take place in the parish. The ghostly bell, heard only by Mrs Bradshaw had indeed tolled the truth.

Many more times – thirty-one times, it is reported, in two and a half years – Mrs Bradshaw was woken by the bell and each time there was a death in the parish next day. It was, to say the least, uncanny.

In those two and a half years, however, Mrs Bradshaw met Ignatius a number of times and to her, if to no one else, the situation was clear. Sometimes the spectral form would become visible in the corridor where she had first seen it; at other times it turned up in other parts of the house. Wherever she found it, Mrs Bradshaw took the opportunity to have a conversation with Ignatius, and in this way she slowly pieced together his story.

The monk had lived, it transpired, nearly eight hundred years ago in a monastery that stood on the self-same spot where now Elm Vicarage stands. It had been the monk's task to keep watch at night for floods, which rose fast and unexpectedly from the fens. If a flood came, Ignatius had to give warning by tolling the bell, so waking his sleeping brethren, who would then have time to scramble to safety before the water reached and swamped the monastery.

Sadly, one night Ignatius fell asleep during his lonely and boring watch. And on that night of all nights, the one night when this usually diligent monk failed briefly in his duty, the waters rose, broke their banks and flooded the monastery. Before they knew what was happening, so stealthily and speedily did the water rise, several monks were drowned in their beds. Poor Ignatius never recovered from the guilt he felt at his failure to give warning. He lived and died a restless soul, and his ghost, it seems, was doomed to walk for ever the place where in life he had made such a tragic error.

Until, that is, seven hundred years later, when Mrs Bradshaw brushed against him in that gloomy corridor. This was the beginning of Ignatius' release from eternal bondage.

One September night Mrs Bradshaw had decided for some reason to sleep on her own in a guest room. With her was the family dog, who was in the habit of spending the night at Mrs Bradshaw's feet. On this particular night, however, the dog seemed uneasy; he whimpered and whined in a nervous, fearful way. Suddenly he fled from the room. Mrs Bradshaw went after him and brought him back. But twice more he scurried off, and only after a great deal of petting and affection would he stay put.

When the dog was calm again, Mrs Bradshaw got into bed, put out the light and went off to sleep. She woke sometime later with the awful feeling that something was being tied round her neck. She grabbed up a torch from her bedside table, switched it on, and found that a tendril of wisteria (a climbing plant that grew outside the room) had somehow got in through the open window and had fallen, snake-like, across her throat. Relieved, she brushed the thing away.

At that very moment, the bedclothes were thrown from her by an invisible force.

Already shocked from waking so abruptly at the touch of the wisteria, thinking that she was being strangled, Mrs Bradshaw was sent by this last event into a fit of terror. But before she could do anything, she felt herself picked violently up and hurled across the bed. This knocked the breath from her, and though she tried instinctively to scream for help, she could not utter a sound.

Worse was to follow. Having had the bedclothes pulled from her and then having been herself lifted bodily into the air and tossed down as though she were no heavier than a feather, she now saw a black and shapeless form appear, towering over her. And from that ugly shape came two gnarled hands which reached out to clutch her by the neck. She tried again to shout for help, but could not; she tried to struggle, but found herself firmly held down by the unyielding hands, which began to tighten their grip till the pain was almost unbearable and she was sure she must soon choke from the pressure.

At this vital moment, Ignatius came into view, walking towards the bed. He stepped forward, took the two gnarled and strangling hands in his own and dragged them away from Mrs Bradshaw's throat.

For a second or two the rector's stricken wife had a chance to catch her breath. But she had little time to recover her wits for she became aware that the malicious form was returning, bending down again towards her. And this time she could make out a huge and bloated head with a hideous red face above the twisted hands. There was never any doubt of the monster's evil intention. While at her side her dog was battling in a frenzy, snarling and biting at something that to Mrs Bradshaw was invisible.

As the malevolent ghost loomed over her body, Mrs Bradshaw managed to summon her last re-

'As the malevolent ghost loomed over her body, Mrs Bradshaw flung herself to one side . . .'

sources of will and energy. She flung herself to one side, tumbled off the bed, and ran to her husband, who was sleeping quite undisturbed in the room the couple usually occupied. He had heard nothing of the struggle, and might have thought the poor woman had suffered no more than a nasty nightmare but for the fact that plainly visible on her neck were such appalling bruises that no one could possibly doubt that, whatever had caused them, Mrs Bradshaw had been through something very much worse than a bad dream. The bruises remained for days afterwards, a witness to that ghastly night.

Next day, Mrs Bradshaw had a meeting with Ignatius. The ghost-monk told her that many years ago a man had been murdered in the room where she had slept the night before. From that time on, the haunted room was kept locked and left unused.

One more thing Ignatius told his friend. Because he had helped to save her life he expected to feel some easing of his guilt, the bond that kept him tied to the mortal earth. Henceforth, he said, Mrs Bradshaw would see less of him.

And so it turned out, until by now Ignatius rests at last in peace.

CHAPTER FIVE

Ghost or guile?
The haunting of Syderstone

Many so-called 'true' ghost stories are little more than legends. The facts in which they had their beginnings have long since been buried under a mountain of trimmings and verbal decoration built up by one story-teller after another to make the stories more exciting, more eerie, more entertaining than they really are. Uncovering the facts can be fascinating detective work. And when the tangled tracery of fiction and invention has been cleared away and you have come as close as possible to the original first-hand accounts, these also need sifting, for no two people witnessing the same event ever give quite the same account of it. You need only compare any two news reports of the same accident to find this out. And if this is true of ordinary, everyday, quite straightforward happenings, how much more likely it must be that people who get mixed up with the extraordinary, unusual and far from straightforward occurrence of a ghost out haunting will tell differing stories about their experience.

Take, for example, the haunting of Syderstone Rectory in Norfolk. The house is near the site where Syderstone Hall once stood. Amy Robsart lived there until she married Robert Dudley, who became Earl

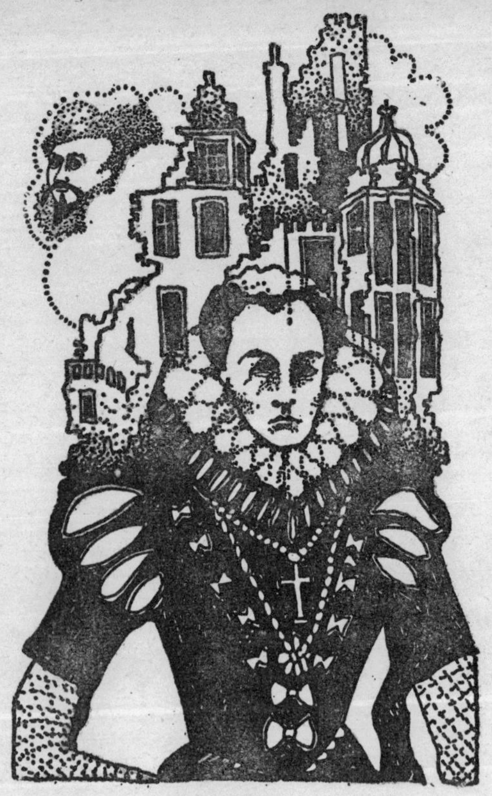

Amy Robsart

of Leicester in Queen Elizabeth's reign. Good Queen Bess liked the handsome young earl and made a favourite of him for a time; so much of a favourite, in fact, that some suspicious folk believed that the earl and his queen wanted to rid themselves of poor Amy and so had her murdered, not at Syderstone but at Cumnor Hall, Berkshire.

Whatever the truth is, Amy Robsart's ghost is supposed to have returned to the house where she was born, there to walk in sorrow until the Hall was demolished, after which the homeless apparition moved to the nearby rectory.

Strange things have been seen there, goings-on that reached a climax in 1833. But instead of retelling the tale, I have presented below the evidence as it can be discovered in articles and newspapers published at the time, so that you can do your own detective work and decide for yourself whether you think, as some people do, that the whole affair was caused by a ghost or, as others believe, that it was nothing more than trickery played on witnesses gullible enough to be taken in. Sometimes the accounts are long-winded and so I have cut bits out if no new information is given. Three dots (. . .) show where this has been done.

The public first heard of the haunting from a newspaper report which appeared in the *Norfolk Chronicle* on June 1st, 1833, sixteen days after the events described:

A REAL GHOST

The following circumstance has been creating some agitation in the neighbourhood of Fakenham for the last few weeks.

In Syderstone Parsonage lives the Rev. Mr. Stewart, curate, and rector of Thwaite. About six weeks since, an unaccountable knocking was heard in it in the middle of the night. The family became alarmed, not being able to discover the cause. Since then it has gradually been becoming more violent, until it has now arrived at such a frightful pitch that one of the servants has left through absolute terror.

The noises commence almost every morning about two, and continue until daylight. Sometimes it is a knocking, now in the ceiling overhead, now in the wall, and now directly under the feet; sometimes it is a low moaning, which the Rev. Gentleman says reminds him very much of the moans of a soldier being whipped; and sometimes it is like the sounding of brass, the rattling of iron, or the clashing of earthenware or glass; but nothing in the house is disturbed. It never speaks, but will beat to a lively tune and moan at a solemn one, especially at the morning and evening hymns. Every part of the house has been carefully examined, to see that no one could be secreted, and the doors and windows are always fastened with the greatest caution. Both the inside and outside of the house have been carefully examined during the time of the noises, which always arouse the family from their slumbers, and oblige them to get up; but nothing has been discovered.

It is heard by everyone present, and several ladies and gentlemen in the neighbourhood who, to satisfy themselves, have remained all night with Mr. Stewart's family, have heard the noise, and have been equally surprised and frightened. Mr. Stewart has also offered any of the tradespeople in the village an opportunity of remaining in the house and convincing themselves. The shrieking last Wednesday week was terrific.

It was formerly reported in the village that the house was haunted by a Rev. Gentleman, whose name was Mantle, who died there about twenty-seven years since, and this is now generally believed to be the case. His vault, in the inside of the church, has lately been repaired, and a new stone put down. The house is adjoining the churchyard, which has added . . . to the horror which pervades the villagers . . .

On Wednesday night Mr. Stewart requested several most respectable gentlemen to sit all night – namely, the Rev. Mr. Spurgin of Docking, the Rev. Mr. Goggs of Creake, the Rev. Mr. Lloyd of Massingham, the Rev. Mr. Titlow of Norwich, and Mr. Banks, surgeon of Holt, and also Mrs. Spurgin. Especial care was taken that no tricks should be played by the servants; but as if to give the visitors a grand treat, the noises were even louder and of longer continuance than usual. The first commencement was in the bedchamber of Miss Stewart, and seemed like the clawing of a voracious animal after its prey. Mrs. Spurgin was at the moment leaning against the bedpost, and the effect on all present was like a shock of electricity. The bed was on all sides clear from the wall; but nothing was visible. Three powerful knocks were then given to the side board [of the bed], whilst the hand of Mr. Goggs was upon it. The disturber was conjured to speak, but answered only by a low hollow moaning; but on being requested to give three knocks, it gave three most tremendous blows apparently in the wall.

The noises, some of which were as loud as those of a hammer on the anvil, lasted from between eleven and twelve o'clock until near two hours of sunrise. The following is the account given by one of the gentlemen: 'We all heard distinct sounds of various kinds – from various parts of the room and the air – in the midst of us – nay, we felt the vibrations of parts of the bed as struck; but we were quite unable to assign any possible natural cause as producing all or any part of this. We had a variety of thoughts and explanations passing in our minds *before* we were on the spot, but we left all equally bewildered.'

On another night the family collected in a room where the noise had never been heard; the maid-servants sat sewing round a table, under the especial notice of Mrs. Stewart, and the man-servant, with his legs crossed and his hands upon his knees, under the cognizance of his master. The noise was then for the first time heard there – 'above, around, beneath, confusion all' – but nothing seen, nothing disturbed, nothing felt except a vibratory agitation of the air, or a tremulous movement of the tables or what was upon them.

This report at once let loose a hornet's nest of disagreement and curiosity. One of the people present during the events on the night of May 15th and named by the newspaper, Mr Spurgin, resented having his name linked to the affair 'without my consent or knowledge', and he wrote to the *Chronicle*'s editor to tell him so, setting right some errors of fact at the same time:

Docking,
June 5th, 1833.

... It is most true that, at the request of the Rev. Mr. Stewart, I was at the parsonage at Syderstone, on the night of the 15th May, for the purpose of investigating the cause of the several interruptions to which Mr. Stewart and his family have been subject for the last three or four months. I feel it right, therefore, to correct some of the erroneous impressions which the paragraph in question is calculated to make upon the public mind, and at the same time to state fairly the leading circumstances which transpired that night.

At ten minutes before two in the morning, 'knocks' were distinctly heard; they continued at intervals, until after sunrise – sometimes proceeding from the bed's-head, sometimes from the side boards of the children's bed, sometimes from a three-inch partition separating the children's sleeping-rooms – both sides of which partition were open to observation. On two or three occasions, also, when a definite number of blows was requested to be given, the precise number required was distinctly heard. *How* these blows were occasioned was the subject of diligent search; every object was before us, but nothing satisfactory to account for them; no trace of any human hand, or of mechanical power, was to be discovered. Still, I would remark, though perfectly distinct, these knocks were by no means so powerful as your paragraph represents – indeed, instead of *being even louder, and of longer continuance that night*, as if to give *the visitors a grand treat*, it would seem they were neither *so* loud nor *so* frequent as they commonly had been. In several instances they were particularly gentle, and the pauses between them afforded all who were present the opportunity of exercising the most calm judgement and deliberate investigation.

I would next notice the *vibrations* on the side board and post of the children's beds. These were distinctly felt by myself as well as others, not only once, but frequently. They were obviously the effect of different blows, given in some way or other, upon the different parts of the beds, in several instances while those parts were actually under our hands. It is not true that *the effect on all present was like a shock of electricity,* but that these *vibrations* did take place, and that too in beds perfectly disjointed from every wall, was obvious to our senses; though in what way they were occasioned could not be developed.

Again – our attention was directed at different times during the night to certain sounds on the bed's head and walls, resembling the scratchings of two or three fingers; but in *no* instance were they *the clawing of a voracious animal after its prey.* During the night I happened to leave the spot in which the party were assembled, and to wander in the dark to some more distant room in the house, occupied by no one member of the family (but where the disturbances originally arose), and there to my astonishment, the same scratchings were to be heard.

At another time, also, when one of Mr. Stewart's children was requested to hum a lively air, *most scientific beatings* to every note were distinctly heard from the bed-head; and at its close, *four blows* were given, louder (I think) and more rapid than any which had before occurred.

Neither ought I to omit that, at the commencement of the noises, several feeble *moans* were heard. This happened more than once; after a time they increased to a series of *groanings* of a peculiarly distressing character, and proceeding (as it seemed) from the bed of one of Mr. Stewart's children, about ten years of age. From the tone of voice, as well as other circumstances, my own conviction is, that these *moans* could not arise from any effort on the part of the child. Perhaps there were others present who might have had different impressions; but be this as it may, towards daybreak four or six shrieks were heard – not from any bed or wall, but as hovering in the atmosphere of the room, where the other noises had been principally heard. These screams were distinctly heard by *all*, but their cause was discoverable by *none.*

These, sir, are the chief events which occurred at Syderstone Parsonage on the night alluded to in your paragraph. I understand the *knockings* and *sounds* have varied considerably in their character on different nights, and that there have been several nights occurring (at four distinct periods) in which *no noises* have been heard.

I have simply related what took place under my own observation. You will perceive that the noises heard by us were by no means so loud and violent as would be gathered from the representations which have been made. Still, as you are aware, they are not on that account the less real; nor do they, on that account, require the less rational explanation.

Mr Spurgin, having stated the facts as he knew them – facts often very different from those given in the newspaper's first report – finished his letter with some information about further investigations that had been carried out at Syderstone since May 15th:

A *trench* was dug round the back part of the house, and *borings* were resorted to in all other parts of it to the depth of six or seven feet, completing a chain round the entire buildings, for the purpose of discovering any subterranean communication with the walls, which aught possibly explain the noises in question. Many parts of the interior of the house, also, such as *the walls, floors, false roofs*, etc., have been minutely examined, but nothing has been found to throw any light upon the source of the disturbances. Indeed, I understand the *knockings* within the last four days, so far from having subsided, are becoming increasingly distressing to Mr. Stewart and his family . . .

Mr Spurgin was clearly in two minds about the haunting; he emphasizes that no explanation could be discovered about *how* the noises were caused, but he was obviously also very impressed by them. Another of the watchers who sat through that chilling night of May 15th yas less worried. This time Mr Titlow in whose opinion the entire performance was a fake. Having read the *Norfolk Chronicle*'s account, he wrote to the editor and told him so; his letter, written on the same day that Mr Spurgin's was published, appeared in the paper on June 8th, 1833.

Norwich,
June 5th, 1833.

Sir: The detail of circumstances connected with the Syderstone Ghost, as reported in the public papers, is in my opinion very incorrect, and calculated to deceive the public. If the report of noises heard on other evenings be as much exaggerated as in the report of noises which five other gentlemen and myself heard on Wednesday evening, the 15th May, nothing could be better contrived to foster superstition and to aid deception.

I was spending a few days with a friend in the neighbourhood of Syderstone, and was courteously invited by Mr. Stewart to sit up at the Parsonage; but I never imagined the noises I heard during the night would become a subject of general conversation in our city and county. As such is the case . . . I hope you will afford the convenience of correcting . . . some of the errors . . .

The noises were *not loud* . . . commenced . . . at about half past one o'clock AM . . .

I heard a scream as of a female, but I was not alarmed; I cannot speak *positively* as to the origin of the scream, but I cannot deny that such a scream may be produced by a ventriloquist. The family are highly respectable, and I know not any good reason for a suspicion to be excited against any one of the members; but as far as it is *possible* for one or two of the members of a family to cause disturbances to the rest, I must confess that I should be more satisfied that there is not a connexion between the ghost and a member of the family if the noises were distinctly heard in the rooms when *all* the members of the family were known to be at a distance from them . . .

I do not deny the existence of supernatural agency, or of its occasional manifestation; but I firmly believe such a manifestation does not take place without Divine permission, and when permitted it is not for trifling purposes nor accompanied with *trifling effects.* Now there are effects which appear to me *trifling*, connected with the noises at Syderstone, and which therefore tend to satisfy my mind that they are *not caused by supernatural agency.* On one occasion the ghost was desired to give ten knocks; he gave nine, and, as if recollecting himself that the number was not complete, he began again and gave ten . . .

If therefore I may express an opinion, that if two or three active and experienced police officers

> from Norwich were permitted to be the sole occupants in the house for a few nights, the ghost would not interrupt their slumbers, or, if he attempted to do it, they would quickly find him out, and teach him better manners for the future ... I am, Sir, your humble servant,
>
> Samuel Titlow

Mr Titlow was, then, no believer in ghosts; the haunting was all nonsense and needed only a couple of burly bobbies to prove it. This sceptical reaction upset Mr Spurgin, who wrote again to the *Chronicle*, pouring scorn on Mr Titlow's suggestion of trickery, reaffirming his belief that the noises could not have been faked, and mentioning one piece of his evidence which seems to answer Mr Titlow's requirement that *all* members of the family should be removed from the noise before anyone could say the noises were supernaturally caused. His letter appeared on June 15th, 1833, and, in part, said:

> I feel myself called on to state publicly that although a diligent observer of the different events which then took place, I witnessed no one circumstance which could induce *me* to indulge a conjecture that the *knocks, vibrations, scratchings, groanings*, etc., which I heard proceeded from any member of Mr. Stewart's family through the medium of mechanical or other trickery – indeed, it would seem to me utterly impossible that the scratchings which fell under my observation during the night, in a remote room of the house,

could be *so* produced, as, at that time, every member of Mr. Stewart's family was removed a considerable distance from the spot.

Having thus disposed of one of Mr Titlow's arguments, Mr Spurgin concluded his letter with some news, which, if it proved to be true, would completely answer Mr Titlow's accusation that the haunting was a trick played by one of the Stewart family:

> Perhaps, Mr. Editor, your distant readers may not be aware that Mr. Stewart has not been resident at Syderstone more than fourteen months, while mysterious noises are *now* proved to have been heard in this house, at different intervals and in different degrees of violence, for the last thirty years and upwards.

Before going on to look at the proof Mr Spurgin mentions, it is as well to summarize the story so far, so that the outline of the facts, as best they can be known, is clear.

The Reverend Stewart and his family went to live in Syderstone Rectory one year and two months before the *Norfolk Chronicle* printed its story about the haunting. Almost immediately, it seems, Mr Stewart, his wife, the children and servants began to hear strange noises which, so far as they could discover, had no natural cause. They told their friends about these disturbing events and to their dismay, the house was soon being visited by streams of curious people who wanted to witness for themselves the ghostly activity. In the end, the Stewarts grew so weary of these invasions of their privacy that they decided to bring together a few people whose opinions they respected and who were likely to have calm judgement to see if they could offer any solution to the problem. This was the party which sat up on the night of May 15th, 1833.

Among those who spent the night in the haunted rectory, we know that Mr Spurgin was convinced that the noises had no human origin, and that Mr Titlow came to just the opposite opinion, believing the haunting to be a trick played by one of the Stewart family.

By this time, Mr Stewart was so fed up with the publicity he refused to make any further statements about the affair, closed his doors to strangers and kept mum; all he wanted was to forget the entire unpleasant business. But he sincerely believed the house, and one bedroom in particular, to be inhabited by a poltergeist (a 'noise-ghost' – a spirit that makes strange sounds and may even throw things about but which is never seen). What is more, Mr Titlow's accusations (and, no doubt, other people's too) against the honesty of his family stuck in his gorge and he decided something must be done to clear the family name. The only thing that could be done was to show that the haunting had been going on in the house *before* the family arrived fourteen months previously.

Very quickly plenty of evidence was turned up among local people who had lived in the area a long time, and who claimed to have had strange experiences at Syderstone. Some of these agreed to swear on oath that their testimony was true. Unfortunately, some of the witnesses could not write, and so their statements had to be taken down at their dictation and signed by each with his own mark – usually a cross. In days gone by when many people could neither read nor write this was the way in which written documents of a legal kind had to be prepared. At the end of each signed statement two men of standing in the community certified that the witness was of good character and honesty of life. The two men who signed the Syderstone documents were Thomas Seppings and John Savory.

The sworn statements were published in the *Norfolk Chronicle* on June 22nd, 1833. There were seven in all, six of the witnesses came from Syderstone, the other from Docking (where, it will be remembered, Mr Spurgin was vicar). The first of these seven pieces of evidence I give below in full because it is interesting to read the old legal language in which it is written. The rest I have shortened, giving only the parts which tell the important details of each story, and omitting the legal declarations.

Elizabeth Goff, whose statement begins the new evidence, had known about ghostly disturbances at Syderstone since 1785, thirty-eight years before Mr Stewart arrived in the parish. She had been a servant to the then rector, the Rev William Mantle. If Elizabeth's account is a true one, then the ghost – if ghost it was – could not have been Mr Mantle's, as the *Chronicle* suggested in its first article, for Mr Mantle was alive at the time!

> Elizabeth Goff, of Docking, in the county of Norfolk, widow, now voluntarily declareth, and is prepared at any time to confirm the same on oath, and say: That she entered into the service of the Rev. William Mantle about the month of April, 1785, at which time her said master removed from Docking to the Parsonage at Syderstone, and the said Elizabeth Goff further states, that at the time of entering upon the said parsonage, two of the sleeping rooms therein were nailed up: and upon one occasion, during the six months of her continuance in the service of her said master, she well remembers the whole family were much alarmed in consequence of Mrs. Mantle's sister having either seen or heard something very unusual in one of the sleeping rooms over the kitchen, which had greatly terrified her. This Declaration was made and signed this 18th day of June 1833 before me, Derek Hoste, one of His Majesty's Justices of the Peace for the County of Norfolk.
>
> *The mark (X) of Elizabeth Goff*

Elizabeth Parsons was next. She was wife to George Parsons, the Syderstone blacksmith, whom she married in 1814. They rented the south end of the rectory and lived there for nine and a half years. Elizabeth had been brought up in Fakenham and had never heard about the hauntings. But after nine or ten months of living in the rectory she was woken one night by some 'very violent and very rapid knocks' in the room immediately underneath the bedroom. She thought the noise was made on the stove and that it had been hit so hard that it must have been broken in pieces. In great fear she woke her husband who then heard the sound too, immediately got up, lit a lamp, and went downstairs to investigate. George found nothing disturbed and no one nor any animal to account for the noise: all was safe and just as it should be. So he returned to bed, put out the light, and lay down again. But at once 'the same blows returned; and were heard by both of them a considerable time'. Mrs Parsons thought she would die from fear.

Almost a year afterwards, Elizabeth was confined to bed because she was about to give birth to a baby. At midnight she heard again strange noises from the room below, noises like the windows being thrown up and the shutters burst open, as well as 'the crashing of chairs placed by the windows'. A nurse was with Elizabeth that night. She hurried down to examine the room below, but, as before, everything was entirely in order.

From time to time throughout her nine and a half years of life in the rectory, Elizabeth was 'constantly interrupted by very frightful and unusual knockings, various and irregular; sometimes they were heard in one part of the house, and sometimes in another; sometimes they were frequent, and sometimes two or three weeks or months or even twelve months would pass without any knock being heard; . . . just at the time she hoped she had got rid of them, they returned to the house, with increased violence'.

Next to give testimony was a friend of the Parsons, a carpenter called Thomas Mase. Sometime in 1820 he was spending a night with the blacksmith and his wife in their 'flat' in the rectory and was sleeping in the attic room, when

> . . . about midnight he heard (he thinks he was awoke out of sleep) a dreadful noise, like the sudden and heavy fall of part of the chimney upon the stove in the lower sitting-room. That crash was so great that, although at a considerable distance from the spot, he distinctly heard the noise, not doubting that the chimney had fallen and dashed the stove to pieces: that he arose and went down-stairs (it being a light summer's night): but upon examining the state of the room and stove, he found, to his astonishment, everything as it ought to have been.

Five or six years later, Thomas was again staying with his friends, sleeping this time in a room at the south end of the rectory. The door of his room must have dropped a little on its hinges; at any rate, when it opened it scraped loudly on the floor and had to be pushed very hard to make it move at all. In the middle of the night, Thomas clearly heard all the noises he associated with the opening of his bedroom door. But when he got up to close it, he found the door shut, just as he had left it when he came to bed earlier in the evening.

About 1824 William Ofield was a gardener at Syderstone Parsonage, and his remembrances of the house come next. William's story is especially interesting, because it is the first account we get of a haunting during daylight hours. It appears he was sitting in the kitchen one day when he heard 'in the bedroom immediately over his head, a noise resembling the dragging of furniture about the room, accompanied with the fall as of some heavy substance upon the floor'. Apparently everyone in the house heard the noise, for the family and servants were all frightened and sent William upstairs to investigate. Of course, as usual, nothing was out of place, and no one was there.

Mr Ofield heard many other noises during his employment at the rectory, noises like the rattling of china and glass in a cabinet, for example; but nothing was ever found that would explain the commotion.

Elizabeth Hooks was a servant in the house from about 1826 till 1830; she testified to hearing sounds like those of moving and rattling furniture, loud knocks from the ceiling in the attic and from the hall door, and once something in a passage 'like a person walking with a peculiar hop'.

One night in 1823 another servant, Phoebe Steward, was left in charge of the rectory. She heard, at about eight o'clock in the evening, what sounded to her like 'people running out of one room into another . . . stumping about very loud', a frightful row that went on for nearly a quarter of an hour. Two years later she again heard footsteps walking from a bedroom down the stairs step by step to the sitting-room door, which she heard open and then a chair near one of the windows moved and the window shutters opened. When she looked round the house all was in order.

A year and a half later while sleeping in the haunted bedroom Phoebe heard 'a very surprising and frightful knock, as if it had struck the head of the bed and dashed it to pieces'. Little wonder that Mrs Steward had 'no hesitation in believing the noises were the work of a ghost'!

Finally comes Robert Hunter's story. Robert was a shepherd employed by Thomas Seppings and he heard stranger noises than anyone else had so far described.

> ... One night in the early part of March 1832, between the hours of ten and eleven o'clock, as he was passing behind the Parsonage at Syderstone in a pathway across the glebe land near the house, when within about twelve yards of the back part of the buildings, his attention was arrested all of a sudden by some very loud 'groanings' like those 'of a dying man – solemn and lamentable', coming as it seemed to him from the centre of the house above: that the said Robert Hunter is satisfied these groans had but then just begun, otherwise he must have heard them long before he approached so near the house. He also further states that the Parsonage at that time was wholly unoccupied, it being about a month before Mr. Stewart's family came into residence there: that these groans made such an impression upon his mind, as he shall never lose to his dying hour. And the said Robert Hunter likewise states, that, after stopping for a

season near the house, and satisfying himself of the reality of these groans, he passed on his way, and continued to hear them as he walked, for the distance of not less than one hundred yards. The said Robert Hunter knows one hundred yards is a great way, yet if he stopped and listened, he doubts not he could have heard them to a still greater distance 'so loud and so fearful were they, that never did he hear the like before'.

This then was the evidence gathered by the Reverend Stewart to support his case and clear his name of fraud. If these seven men and women can be believed then there can be little doubt that something inexplicable had been going on at Syderstone for a very long time. Mr Titlow might well have argued that, nevertheless, the whole thing was trickery, a nasty joke played by some far-from-ghostly human being. But if you accept this explanation, then you have also to accept that someone would have the tenacity to go on playing such a trick for over forty years, and never during all those years be found out.

On the other hand, even if the noises were not caused by someone playing tricks, it does not necessarily follow that they were the work of ghosts. Sometimes the movement of water in underground streams that pass beneath a house unknown to the occupants can cause eerie creaks and groans and set up vibrations (like miniature earthquakes) that cause crockery to rattle, old beds to shake, and ancient timbers to crack apparently without natural cause.

The Syderstone haunting has fascinated many people. Even so, the mystery is unsolved, despite Mr Stewart's strenuous efforts. Was the rectory really inhabited by a ghost? Or were Mr Stewart and his friends – except the sceptical Mr Titlow – taken in by practical jokers or subterranean streams? You must decide for yourself what you believe, for one thing is certain: no one will ever be able to prove conclusively what happened. Ghosts don't care for proof!

CHAPTER SIX

Violet Tweedale's ghosts

Some people seem to be born with psychic powers; if there is a ghost about, they'll see it or hear it or, at the very least, feel its presence when other people who do not have such gifts notice nothing out of the ordinary. Violet Tweedale was such a person. (Before her marriage her name was Chambers, but I'm not, as far as I know, any relation!) Some years ago, she wrote a book called *Ghosts I Have Seen* in which she described her numerous meetings with apparitions.

The very first of these sometimes hair-raising adventures took place outside Broughton Hall, which used to stand on the outskirts of Edinburgh, a 'very grim and forbidding looking place' she says, 'hidden from the eyes of the curious behind very high walls, and was entered upon by two huge gates, always kept closed'. The Hall was occupied then by three eccentric sisters named Walker, their brother Adam, and the servants. Everyone believed the house was dreadfully haunted, but no one would tell what went on.

Apparently Violet's father was fascinated by ghosts and he determined to find out just what spectres inhabited Broughton Hall, which was only a few yards away from the Chambers' own house. At this time – about 1870 – Violet was little more than seven or eight years old, but already she had acquired her father's taste for the supernatural, and he seems to have encouraged his daughter's passion. Together they would prowl quietly round the Hall after dark in hopes of meeting one of the ghosts. These expeditions lasted about half an hour each, and for quite a while father and small daughter had little luck. Then one night their patience was rewarded.

> It was November [Violet Tweedale wrote in her book], dry but wild and bitterly cold. Billowy white snow clouds scudding before a brisk north wind threw us alternately into light and darkness, as they covered and uncovered the face of the full moon. We had emerged from our house about half past nine, and had reached the back of Broughton Hall. The house was shrouded in darkness and dead silence, every blind was close drawn, and the suggestion was one of utter emptiness. My father and I were walking apart, I being right under the shadow of the walls, whilst he was in the middle of the paved court, which had neither hedge nor wall, but met the edge of the field running up to it.
>
> Suddenly I heard him whisper 'Hush!' though we never did utter a word whilst close to the house. I stared ahead, and then I saw, clearly lit by the moon, a woman who had apparently just rounded the corner of the house. She was running hard, straight towards us, and her feet made no sound on the round cobble stones.
>
> Terror suddenly seized me, and I darted across to my father, and got well behind him, seizing him

finally round the waist. The woman came on, rushing wildly. She had nearly reached us, and I was almost thrown over as my father faced her, and backed to allow her to pass. I peered round him, and saw a woman, ghastly pale, and distraught-looking, clad in a white nightdress. Two long strands of black hair streamed out behind her, and her bare arms were outstretched in front. In a flash she had passed, and absolutely silently, and I found myself lying on the ground alone, and my father vanishing in hot pursuit.

Needless to say I very quickly picked myself up again, and joined in the chase. Terror lent me wings, and in a minute or two I came up with him, standing breathless by the gate.

'Vanished into thin air just as I reached her. That's always the way. You can't catch them,' he said.

We made a little détour before going home, in order to discuss the great event. We had no doubt that we had seen a genuine apparition. We knew all the occupants of the Hall, and the woman had vanished in the open, and in full flight, just as my father had come alongside her.

Violet Tweedale gives no explanation for the wild, running woman in a nightdress, the first of all the ghosts she saw. But before she was much older, she encountered her second spirit, once again when with her father, and this time there was a story about it, known to those present with Violet at the haunting.

Mr Chambers had taken his daughter to visit a very old woman who lived alone, tended by a servant, in an ancient house in Inveresk. Again the building was surrounded by high walls that cut it off from the road and the people outside; and behind the walls was a beautiful garden.

The old woman gave her visitors 'a delicious tea, consisting of fresh baked scones, butter made of real cream – margarine was not then invented – home-made strawberry jam, and home-laid eggs'. It was a glorious spring evening and all three sat by an open window so that the perfume from the lilacs and wallflowers and lilies of the valley, which crowded the garden, drifted into the room.

Now each time they went to tea with this old woman, Mr Chambers always asked, 'Have you seen her again?' Sometimes the answer given by the old woman would be Yes, sometimes No. Violet gathered that this question referred to the woman's dead daughter, her only child. The daughter had been violently insane for many years, and had been cared for by her mother – a difficult task – until she died aged fifty-five, leaving the mother alone.

That afternoon at tea, Violet's father asked his question as usual; but no sooner had he spoken the words when, Violet wrote:

. . . he broke off the conversation.

'My God! There she is!' He half rose from his chair and stared through the open window. I looked in the same direction. A woman was strolling aimlessly along the path just outside. There was a curious uncertainty about her movements. She walked like a blind person, who has neither stick nor arm to guide her. Strangely enough I never thought of connecting this woman with the ghost of the mad daughter. She looked so natural, so commonplace. Her hollow face was quite grey, and her dark hair was drawn tightly back from it, and rolled in an ugly knob behind. Her dress was of some dark material, her boots were of cloth, and her hands and arms were rolled up in an apron she wore.

There she was, vacantly wandering in the garden, in the lovely spring evening, with the blackbirds and thrushes singing their hearts out all round her . . .

I turned round to say something to the old woman . . . She had gone down on her knees, and had hidden herself by throwing the end of the tablecloth over her head.

Then I turned my eyes back to the apparition. I don't suppose she was visible for more than four minutes. I remember Father uttering consoling words to the effect that 'she's gone', and helping the old woman into her chair again, when we resumed our tea and conversation, as if nothing unusual had occurred.

It is not surprising that after such a haunted start to her life, Violet Tweedale was for ever afterwards an avid ghost hunter, and a very successful one too, if her book is to be believed. Long after these two childhood events, when she had grown up, she met a ghost which, despite her experience of tangling with the supernatural, frightened her considerably. This is how she tells the story:

In the year 1900 we took a house for the winter months in the West End of London.

It was a small house though joined on either side by great mansions, and once upon a time it had actually been a farmhouse standing amid smiling fields.

It retained many relics of its ancient origin, and had been for many of its latter years the town residence of a man whose type has practically died out, the perfect type of our old English aristocracy.

The bedroom I occupied was exceedingly comfortable and warm. The bed, placed against the wall, was exactly opposite to the fireplace, so that lying on my right side I looked straight at the fire and could see the whole room.

I was constantly on the alert, as I knew how full of history such a house must be, but for several weeks I neither saw nor heard anything in the least unusual.

One night, quite unexpectedly, a change occurred. I no longer had the room to myself. A stranger occupied it with me.

It was a cold, snowy night, and I was lying in bed facing the fire and courting sleep, when I heard a sudden noise which was totally different to the sounds made by a dying fire. Take a large sheet of stiff writing paper in your hand and crush it up between your fingers and you will hear the sound I heard. Quite a loud and distinct noise if you happen to be in a very quiet room, at an hour when all the household has retired to bed.

Naturally, I instantly opened my eyes and looked out into the room, which was lit brightly enough by the fire to make all the objects it contained quite distinct.

An armchair was drawn up close to the fire; half an hour before I had been seated in it warming my toes before getting into bed; now it was again filled.

In it sat a man turned sideways towards me. He was lying back with his legs stretched straight out in front of him towards the fire. One of his arms hung over the arm of the chair, and in his clenched hand was a large piece of paper or parchment.

His finely cut profile was clearly outlined, he was clean shaven, and he stared into the fire, his chin sunk in a high black collar.

His hair was powdered and tied behind by a large black bow, and he wore bright blue cloth knee breeches, white stockings, silver buckled shoes, and many gold buttons on his blue coat. I did not take in all those details at once, I had ample leisure to do so later. For, I suppose, a full two minutes I stared very hard at him, and lay very still, knowing full well I was looking at a ghost. Then very cautiously I drew the bedclothes over my head, and shut out the startling vision. I was invaded by wild panic.

I have never been one of those timid women who

'In it sat a man turned sideways towards me . . .'

are frightened by their own shadows. I require to be face to face with a tangible danger before I put faith in its existence, yet I confess that at that moment I knew what actual fear meant. My heart beat thickly, then seemed to stop, and I was instantly bathed in cold perspiration. I knew that the servants were all in bed two flights of stairs below me, and my husband was out of London, so calling for help was no use. I therefore forced a sort of spurious desperate courage, and began to be angry with myself for being thus afraid when no cause for fear existed. I treated myself to a scornful lecture. 'You who profess to know all about ghosts, you who have actually seen several ghosts, you coward to quail before this one! Don't you know perfectly well that he won't hurt you, and he has a perfect right to sit in that chair, and that it is your duty to speak to him should he show any desire for conversation.'

'I am terribly alone,' pleaded my other self in feeble self-defence.

'Well, what of it? If the whole household was in the room what could they do? You are not a child. Uncover your head and look the spectre boldly in the face.'

The stillness and hush of deep night, at the hour when sleepers slumber soundest, was upon the house. The traffic of London was muffled in a heavy fall of snow. I could hear nothing but the feeble crackling of the fire, but gradually I rallied my courage and faculties, and peeped stealthily out.

There sat that dark form between me and the fire; there he lay in an attitude of moody carelessness, watching the cooling embers as they faded from scarlet to pink, from pink to yellow, and then fell tinkling into heaps of white ashes. No statue was ever stiller. He did not move in the least, but sat more like an effigy of a man carved out of stone than a creature of flesh and blood.

I closed my eyes and re-opened them, to test the fact whether I was awake or asleep and dreaming. No, I was broad awake and the room was still fairly well lit, and there sat the phantom before the fire, the proud, well-set head with its powdered curls distinctly visible in the red glow of the firelight. I should think an hour must have passed thus, whilst I gazed at the figure before me, taking in every detail. There was no indication that he knew or cared for my presence. The figure sat like a stone.

I came to the conclusion that the phantom was about thirty years of age, and a sailor who had lived in the days of Nelson, judging by his clothes and the pictures I had seen. I noticed particularly his hand clenched on the paper. A white hand, with strong cruel-looking fingers. There is so much character in hands. The face may be drilled into a mere mask, but hands tell tales of their owners. I could imagine the hands that had crushed the paper closing, murderous, on the throat of an adversary, or gripped hard on the hilt of a dagger.

There were moments when the awful inertia of the figure began to play havoc with my nerves, when I would have given anything to make that impassive form move from out its dreary attitude of sullen brooding; anything to cause the profile of the face, with all its gloom and pride, to turn and front me, so that I might know the worst. But the figure never turned, never stirred, but sat with stately head bowed under a weight of thought.

Now and again a little flame would spurt up and glitter on his shoe buckles, his brass buttons, but the fire was dying now, and gradually the figure became more and more indistinct.

Then I slept. I had been feeling drowsy for some time, and fought against it. I had violently resisted sleep, feeling a great repugnance to losing consciousness whilst the spectre still sat there, but the blank force of sleep at length overpowered me. When I woke the cold grey morning light was stealing feebly in through the window. The chair was empty. The figure was gone.

The next night I went to bed full of courage, but I was left alone. If the sailor returned it was not until after I had gone to sleep.

A week later he came back. One moment the chair was empty, the next moment with one wild heart throb I opened my eyes at the sound of crackling paper, and the chair was filled. There he sat in his brooding sullen attitude and continued to sit till slumber vanquished me. After that I saw him at constant intervals.

By this time I had entirely rid myself of all fear. I did not even desire to change my room, which would have been very inconvenient, and I dreaded alarming the household and being left alone to conduct the domestic duties. But though no longer afraid those constant visits began to get on my nerves, and I consulted a Catholic friend who was always sympathetic to the occult side of life.

She said at once that this spirit should be exorcised and set free from the bondage of earth, and that she had an old friend, a Franciscan monk, who was known to be a powerful exorcist. She offered to arrange the matter, and I gladly accepted her suggestion.

It was on an early spring afternoon that Father Reginald Buckler came to the house. In his white habit,* sandalled feet and shorn crown, he looked an incongruous figure in that fashionable locality already beginning its social entertainments in view of the season's approach. He was a charming, courteous old man, who took his mission very seriously. After a few words of explanation we mounted to the bedroom floor.

There were four doors opening on to the landing, and without asking which of the doors led to the haunted chamber, he turned the handle of the right one and entered. Still he put no question, but at once proceeded with the Service of Exorcism.

Sprinkling the four corners of the room with Holy Water, he bade me kneel down in the middle. Then he raised his crucifix and offered up prayers for the repose of the earth-bound soul, that he might be loosed and set free.

* Violet Tweedale may have made a mistake about the monk's order. Franciscans usually wear brown habits.

For five weeks longer we remained in the house, but I never saw the sailor again.

This may have been the end of the ghostly sailor, but it was not the end of Violet Tweedale's meetings with supernatural beings. If you ever see a copy of her book lying unsold in some secondhand bookseller's shop – which is probably the only place you'll discover a copy these days – it is worth the few pence it will cost to have the pleasure of reading the rest of this strange woman's even stranger adventures with spooks and spectres.

CHAPTER SEVEN

The haunting of Ashley Hall

This is the story of the ghost of Ashley Hall, an old house that still stands on the banks of the River Bollen in Cheshire. It was originally told by the young woman who knew all the details to a friend of hers then at Cambridge University. As it happened many years ago, the young woman's language now seems somewhat old fashioned and her account here and there long-winded. So I have retold her tale in words she might have used were she alive and writing today. But all the important details are just as she recorded them.

When I had just left school I went with my best friend, Miss Meredith, on a visit to her mother at Ashley Hall. Mrs Meredith was a wealthy widow, very lively and great fun. She laughed a lot – I remember that most of all – and she ate a lot too, and was always kind and generous to her guests whom she seemed to enjoy making happy. It is also important to know, because of what happened later, that Mrs Meredith was afraid of nothing. 'I haven't a nerve in my body!' she used to say and then laugh; and it was her constant hope that she would die as she had lived, in luxury and comfort. Altogether, she was

Ashley Hall

the sort of old person I couldn't help liking – lively, gay, not a bit stick-in-the-mud.

When my friend and I arrived, we found the house crowded with guests, so crowded, in fact, that all the usual bedrooms were occupied. Mrs Meredith apologized for having to put me in the Cedar Room, which wasn't really a bedroom at all, but an ante-chamber, a sort of corridor-room with doors leading to different parts of the house. But I didn't mind. It was large and old and had a beautiful high wainscot of cedar wood (from which the room took its name), and it wasn't a bit spooky – there were no dark old pictures or hanging tapestries or bulky bits of furniture to set you imagining strange figures were lingering in the shadows. In fact, there were very few shadows at all, for huge windows let in plenty of light and slid open easily on their sash cords. There was a pleasant fireplace, too, neither over-decorated as the fireplaces in big houses sometimes are, nor too small for this large room.

Beautiful and inviting that room may have looked; but some very strange things went on there. The first I knew about happened that night, though at the time I thought nothing of it.

We had been dancing and I went to bed in high spirits. Tired though I was, however, between two and three o'clock in the night I woke with a start. Quite distinctly I saw a woman's figure passing through my room.

'Who's there?' I called out, feeling no fear, but just a little startled by the sudden intrusion.

I got no answer. The figure walked slowly on its way and disappeared at the door.

This struck me as rather odd; here it was, the middle of the night, and some woman comes traipsing through my room, not even replying when asked a question by the room's rightful occupant. But I knew the house was full of guests, many of whom did not know their way around the many corridors in the big old mansion, and so I naturally supposed that someone going late to bed – perhaps a little tipsy into the bargain – had lost her way in the dark and had stumbled accidentally into my passage-bedroom. The poor woman had probably been too embarrassed to tell me who she was! At any rate, I thought, it will all be cleared up in the morning at breakfast. So I looked at my watch and went back to sleep, not at all alarmed by what had happened.

When I got up next morning the mystery of my late-night visitor deepened, however. As I was dressing I remembered suddenly that before going to bed the night before I had carefully locked all the doors into my room. I checked each lock and found them all safely secured, just as I had left them. How could anyone have got into my room by accident? But someone had done so. I had seen the figure quite clearly by the light of the moon which had shone dimly through the windows. Who could that person have been?

I raced downstairs to breakfast, determined to get to the bottom of the mystery.

Mrs Meredith was already at the table, presiding over the meal as bright and cheerful as always. As soon as I sat down she asked me how I had slept.

'Very soundly,' I said as calmly as I could, 'except that I was rather surprised by someone who, no doubt by mistake, passed through my room at two this morning.'

Mrs Meredith's cheerful smile drifted from her face. She stared at me for a moment; then she began to speak, but suddenly checked herself and turned away from me. No one else at the table seemed to notice the incident, nor did anyone join in the conversation and confess to being the mysterious intruder who had a key to my room. So, for the moment, I decided to let the matter drop.

That night I went to bed earlier than before and was soon fast asleep. But once again at the same hour – about two – I was suddenly wide awake, my eyes staring into the gloom.

The figure was there again, just as on the first night.

Somehow, I found I was expecting it, was waiting, ready to note every detail. And this time, I could see its face. Terrified though I now was, I fixed my eyes on it.

The countenance was dreadful: pale, with large, melancholy, black eyes. And those eyes, along with the noiseless tread as the figure glided over the bare oak floor, gave me a sensation of such deep, deep fear as I shall never forget in all my life, a fear that struck like ice inside me.

For one moment, a moment that seemed endless, the apparition stood in front of me. Then, slowly, it receded. When it reached the middle of that enormous room, it stopped. And then, while I stared at it unblinking, it . . . *was not*. I can find no other way to describe what happened. 'Vanish' sounds like a magician's conjuring trick; 'disappear' does not suggest the stark suddenness of the effect of the figure first being there, then not being there. No single word catches the astonishing truth of what I witnessed.

I must confess the effect of all this upon me was

shattering. For the rest of the night sleep was impossible. I tried to make myself believe that what I had seen was a fantasy, an illusion, a trick my mind played upon me when I was too sleepy to know the difference between reality and dream. I told myself that the figure had gone for good, that I would see it no more. But nothing calmed me, nothing soothed my excited nerves, nothing quelled my shivering fear. I made up my mind that I would leave the house next morning – or, at the very least, insist that Mrs Meredith provide me with another room.

Morning came at last – I felt sometimes that it never would – bright and sunny, and the rising sun shone through my window, finding me sitting up in bed, eyes bleary but quite unable to close in sleep. I got up as soon as I heard other people stirring in the house, washed, dressed and prepared to tackle my hostess. Of course, by then everything that had happened in the night seemed childishly unlikely and silly! How could I go to Mrs Meredith and demand that she move me to another room? Or how could I leave the house without a polite (and believable) explanation? If I told the truth, wouldn't people simply laugh at me and say how ridiculous my story was? I peered round that large and beautiful, airy room and could hardly believe what I nevertheless knew to be the truth.

In the end, I went down to breakfast looking as normally happy as I could and said nothing about my ghost.

The third night came. I must admit, as the evening wore on, I shuddered more and more every time I thought of going to bed. I began to make excuses for staying up later and later. I talked non-stop; I played the piano; I sang; I laughed at everything and anything – and must have seemed either drunk or stupid. I did anything that would help keep me from my room until that dreaded hour – two o'clock – was gone. And I succeeded. When finally I stumbled, exhausted at the effort of the evening, to my room and tumbled into bed, two o'clock was long since past. Even so, I steeled myself against the worst.

Before getting into bed, I had searched every corner, every inch of that huge room. There was nothing unusual, of course. I had bolted and barred every door, and then checked them all. And once in bed, in the moment before I turned out my light, I glanced round, making a final check that all was where it should be. Then I put out the light and flung myself under the bedclothes, head and all.

After lying in this hot and suffocating fashion for nearly two hours in an agony of anticipatory fright, I at last screwed up enough courage to take a hurried glance at the room. It must, I thought, be near daybreak. And it was.

But there also, in the bleak light of early dawn, stood the spectral figure! Not walking, this time, across the room, nor standing at a distance from me in the middle of the floor. But there, right there beside me, her eerie form bent towards my face, her ghastly features – oh, those cavernous, black and melancholy eyes! – so close to me that I could have touched them. The mist-white drapery that covered her form drooped, falling over my trapped body so that had I

'There stood the spectral figure . . .'

been able to move – which I could not, I was so paralysed with fear – I would have disarranged its cascading folds.

For a time – I cannot possibly say how long – I stared, transfixed. Never before – and I hope never again – have I felt so vulnerable, so menaced, so much at the mercy of another being.

And then I fainted.

When I came to, it was almost noon. The servants and finally Mrs Meredith herself, I learned later, had repeatedly knocked at my door, and receiving no reply, decided I was sleeping soundly after my late night, and left me undisturbed. By the time I struggled out of bed and got downstairs, feeling weak and nervous, everyone else had gone off on a day's outing. Except for Mrs Meredith, who sat waiting for me.

Not surprisingly, she was struck by my appearance as soon as she saw me.

'Are you unwell?' she asked, full of concern.

'I think I must be,' I said, my voice trembling, 'and if you will allow me, I think I shall return home this morning.'

For a moment Mrs Meredith looked at me in silence. And then, with such an emphasis that I had no doubt what was in her mind, she said, 'Have you any special reason for going?'

Had I wished to keep my experience to myself, I could not have done. I wanted desperately to talk about it with someone; and there could be no better person than Mrs Meredith. So I sat down and with some relief poured out my story, giving every vivid detail of my three nights of interrupted sleep. She listened gravely and without comment or any sign of the reaction she felt to what I had to tell.

Only when I had finished did she sigh and say, 'I'm deeply sorry about all this, my dear. I've heard strange and inexplicable stories about that room before, but I have always thought they were no more than idle tales and have not believed them. This is the first time in years that the room has been occupied, and I shall never forgive myself for having put you in it.' She paused for a second before going on. 'But for God's sake, my dear, don't mention to anyone else what you have just told me. Promise you won't utter one syllable of it. If the other guests – or the servants – hear even a rumour of such events, why, not one would stay with me. And that would make me very sad.'

Poor Mrs Meredith! The last thing I wanted to do was hurt or offend her. I readily agreed to keep quiet; but though she pressed me to stay longer, I felt I could not spend another night in that house, and so I packed my things at once and went home that morning.

A long time passed before I visited Ashley Hall again. In the interval Miss Meredith, my best and dearest friend, died and her loss distressed me deeply. Finally, I received a pressing invitation from Mrs Meredith to come as a guest to the Hall, and I felt I had to accept. Besides, the memory of my encounter with the ghost had dimmed and I wondered whether it had not been in fact no more than a girlish fancy, something I had now outgrown, but which had seemed real enough at the time and which Mrs Meredith had been kind and understanding enough to treat seriously instead of passing it off with a laugh.

When I arrived, I found Mrs Meredith's sister, Lady Pierrepoint, already there with her three young children. They had spent Christmas together and were having a lively time. If Mrs Meredith was gay, generous and energetic, her sister was domineering, sharp-tongued and strong-willed. She demanded her own way in everything and usually got it. A formidable woman. Which is how it came about that her children were using the Cedar Room as their bedroom. Lady Pierrepoint liked the place and nothing her sister said would put her off from installing the children in it. The one thing which Mrs Meredith could not say, of course, and the one thing that might have changed her sister's mind, was that the room was said to be haunted.

For two weeks all was well. Mrs Meredith stopped worrying about the Cedar Room, began to relax and congratulated herself on the happy turn affairs had taken after all. Perhaps, she thought, the ghost had gone, frightened off maybe by the three bouncy Pierrepoint children and their masterful mother!

Until one day she went into the room and found her nephews packing their playthings.

'What, are you tired of Ashley and going to leave me?' Mrs Meredith asked them cheerily.

'Oh no,' the boys said, 'but we are going to hide our toys from the White Lady. She came last night and Sunday night, and she had such large black eyes and she stood close by the bed – just here, Aunt. Who is she, do you know? She never speaks. What does she do here, and what does she want?'

Mrs Meredith was panic-stricken. So the ghost had not gone after all! And the poor children had seen it! What would her sister do when she found out?

Mrs Meredith could think of one thing only. The children must be put at once into another room. She rang for the housekeeper and set about the operation. Despite puzzled questions from everyone, she braved it out, resisting even her sister's demands to know what was going on, gave no reason for her decision, and against all opposition shifted the Pierrepoint boys out of the Cedar Room.

'God forgive me,' she whispered to me as we worked, 'but I tell you this White Lady will be the death of me.'

After that the haunted room was shut up and for many years I saw Ashley Hall no more. Not until Mrs Meredith's youngest son came of age. Naturally, a great party was held and everyone whom the Merediths knew, from their garden labourer to Lord Pierrepoint, came in during the day to congratulate the young man. Mrs Meredith received them all with her usual grace and charm.

So many people were about that the Cedar Room was opened to provide much needed extra space away from the throng of the guests. At one moment towards evening, Mrs Meredith escaped there to tidy herself up and prepare for the party. The happiness of the day shut out from her mind all thought of ghosts and the White Lady.

In the Cedar Room there was a big, full-length

looking-glass standing near one of the windows. Mrs Meredith put on her evening gown and went to the glass to adjust it and rearrange her hair. As she stood there, looking at herself, she saw to her horror suddenly materialize at her side the ghostly White Lady. For a second they gazed at one another. Then, without uttering a sound, Mrs Meredith collapsed to the floor.

For weeks she was ill. The doctors could not account for her sickness and described it as brain fever. Whatever it was, Mrs Meredith slowly recovered her reason and her memory. But she never recovered her health. Not long afterwards that once light-hearted, loving and lovable woman left Ashley Hall for ever to lie at her husband's side in the family grave.

At her funeral, as I stood unable to restrain my tears at the graveside, I could not help recalling those whispered words: 'God forgive me, but I tell you this White Lady will be the death of me.' They were words that seemed at that moment to have been prophetic.

CHAPTER EIGHT

Mummy's ghost: the haunting of Birchen Bower

Birchen Bower farm used to be in Hollinwood, not far from Oldham and Ashton in Lancashire. The Ferranti factory is there now, covering the site where the farm stood, and, it seems, the ghost that used to haunt the farm has been seen in the works. I came across the story in an old book by John H. Ingram and liked it so much that I at first thought of setting it down here word for word. But then, on second thoughts, I decided that some of Mr Ingram's language might confuse and bore young readers today so I have rewritten the story where the original language seemed tiresome. None of the information has been changed, of course; and at the end I have tacked on a note that brings the tale up to date.

Birchen Bower

ADAPTED FROM J. H. INGRAM'S VERSION

Most accounts of haunted dwellings are connected with some terrible tragedy. The legend of the old haunted house at Birchen Bower, however, has a funny side too. As usual, gold is at the bottom of the story. Whatever the reader believes of the sights and sounds said to belong to Birchen Bower, it cannot be denied that some kind of hereditary trouble belongs to it, as the following particulars (taken chiefly from an article by Mr James Dronsfield in the *Oldham Chronicle* for 1869) will clearly show.

Towards the end of July 1869, a body was buried in Harpurhey Cemetery. The body was the corpse of old Miss Beswick, which, in mummified form, had been on show for many years in the Manchester Museum. For almost a century, so it was said, the rightful heirs of Birchen Bower, Rose Hill, and Cheetwood estates had been prevented from claiming their property by a clever trick. The burial of the mummy would help to restore their lands to the family of the former owners.

The old house, Birchen Bower, was a quaint four-gabled building, shaped like a cross and noted for the beauty of its surroundings in summer. All of it, except for the south wing, was demolished some years ago, but the spirit – or whatever it may be called – did not desert the spot when the place was destroyed.

Miss, or Madame Beswick, as she is often called, is the centre about which all the curious stories gather. Who she really was is uncertain, but the legend says that she lived at Bower House and farmed the land until old age forced her to retire to a little stone cottage which stood on the brink of a mill-stream that rippled through the sloping front garden.

The old lady was supposed to be very wealthy, and when the Scottish rebels led by Prince Charlie came to the neighbourhood in 1745, she was terribly afraid they would take her belongings. So she hid 'vast sums of money and articles of value' in different places on the premises. The Scottish soldiers did not actually reach the farm, but afterwards Miss Beswick's relatives could not persuade her to tell them where she had hidden her treasures. A few days before her death, it is said, she promised that if they would carry her to Bower House she would disclose the secret and point out where the gold was; but the relatives would not do as she asked. Then suddenly Miss Beswick died, leaving the whole affair wrapped in mystery.

For a hundred years Miss Beswick's body was not buried. All kinds of reasons have been given to explain why the interment was so long delayed, but the following account includes the most popular, if not the historically accurate events.

A brother of Miss Beswick, many years before her own death, was supposed to have been thought dead. Everything was prepared for his burial, but just before the coffin-lid was screwed down signs of life were noticed in the corpse. At once everything possible was done to revive the young man, and after lying for several days in a coma, he did at last come back to consciousness to live for many years after. This extraordinary incident made such an impression on his sister's mind that she made a will, leaving all her property to her doctor, Charles White, for as long as he kept her body uncoffined and unburied.

When at last Miss Beswick died – the secret of her hidden treasure still untold – Doctor White embalmed her body and was thus able to keep it out of the ground. In this way he satisfied the conditions of the will and prevented the property from falling into the hands of the Beswick family.

Whatever may be the facts and whatever the fiction in this story it is difficult to say. But the following extract from the *Manchester Guardian* (now the national newspaper, *The Guardian*) of Saturday, August 15th, 1868, confirms some portions of the popular account.

A CURIOUS INTERMENT

On the 22nd of July were committed to the earth in the Harpurhey Cemetery the remains of Miss Beswick, removed from the Peter Street Museum. There is a tradition that this lady, who is supposed to have died about one hundred years ago, had acquired so strong a fear of being buried alive that she left certain property to her (medical?) attendant, so long (so the story runs) as she should be kept above ground. The doctor seems to have embalmed the body with tar, and then swathed it with a strong bandage, leaving the face exposed, and to have kept 'her' out of the grave as long as he could. For many years past the mummy has been lodged in the rooms of the Manchester Natural History Society, where it has long been the object of much popular interest. It seems that the Commissioners who are charged with the re-arrangements of the Society's collections, have deemed this specimen undesirable, and have at last buried it.

One of the strange arrangements Miss Beswick made with her doctor was that every twenty-one years her body should be taken to Birchen Bower and remain there for one week. Old people, who knew about it, declare that the body was indeed taken there at the stipulated times, and put in the granary at the old farmstead. In the morning, these old folk say, when the body was fetched from the granary, the horses and cows kept there were always found let loose. And sometimes a cow would be found up in the hay loft, although how it got there was a mystery as there was no passage large enough to take a beast of such size. The last prank of this sort that we know of was a few years ago when a cow belonging to the farmer then renting the place was found in the hay loft, and it was the belief held by many people that a supernatural being had put it there. Blocks and tackle had to be borrowed from Bower Mill to get the cow down by lowering it through the loading door on the outside wall of the loft.

After Miss Beswick's death her old house was divided into several dwellings. There are many strange stories of the marvellous things seen and heard in them.

One family grew so familiar with the ghost of the old lady, always dressed in a silk gown, that they were never alarmed when it appeared. Sometimes they would be at supper when they would hear a rustle of silk at the front door, and presently the figure of a lady wearing black silk would glide through the room, walk straight into the living-room and then disappear when it reached one particular flagstone on the floor. It was a harmless spirit, annoying no one, and its appearance never caused the family to say anything more than, 'Quiet! The old lady is coming again.'

In another of the dwellings a man had a treadle-lathe for wood-turning, which he used after work for doing odd jobs of joinery for his neighbours. Sometimes he would go into his workroom and find the lathe spinning round at full pelt, kept going by an invisible hand.

Many years ago when flour was a fearful price and bread almost unattainable, the hand-loom weavers, who were then living in the Birchen Bower houses, were starving for lack of food. But one of them, known as Joe at Tamer's, made such large purchases and seemed so flush with money that everyone was puzzled. It was common knowledge that Joe had a large family of small children who depended on Joe's work with his loom for their living. Yet it was obvious that the children were stinted neither for food nor clothes.

Now Joe lived in one wing of the Birchen Bower house, and it was rumoured that he had found the gold hidden by Madame Beswick. Years went by before the source of Joe's wealth was disclosed. Joe then confessed that he had pulled up the floor of the haunted room, intending to build a loom for one of his children,* when he found a tin vessel filled with gold wedges, each worth three pounds ten shillings; a small fortune in those days. He never mentioned this

* I take this haunted room to be the same one which the ghost of the black silk-clothed old lady went into and vanished over the flagstone. A. C.

to anyone, but took the wedges to Oliphant's in St Anne's Square, Manchester, where he sold them. People were still living a few years ago [that is, a few years before 1900 or so] who knew Joe at Tamer's, and the tin box in which he found the gold is said to be still in the hands of his descendants.

It was thought that the discovery of the treasure would break the spell; that Madame's troubled spirit would now rest. But this did not happen. The haunting went on.

Some few years ago she was seen near the old well by the side of the brook when one of the heirs was trying to recover his property. A labourer was going to fetch a pail of water; but when he got to the well he saw a tall lady standing by it wearing a black silk gown and a white cap with a stiff frilly border on it. She stood there in the dusk in a defiant, almost threatening attitude. And streams of blue light seemed to dart from her eyes and flash on the horror-stricken man.

She still troubles the old neighbourhood. On clear, moonlit nights she walks in a headless state in the old barn and the horse pool. At other times the apparition takes the form of various animals. But always it is lost sight of near the pool where the horses drink, which has led some folk to believe that she concealed something there also during the Scottish invasion, which she is trying to point out to anyone courageous enough to speak to her.

On dark and dreary winter nights the barn, it is said, appears to be on fire. A red glare of glowing heat is observed through the loop-holes and crevices of the building, and strange, unearthly noises come from it, as if Satan and all his imps were holding a party there. Sometimes, indeed, the sight is so threatening that the neighbours will raise an alarm and knock up the farmer and tell him the barn is in flames. When the premises are searched, however, nothing is found wrong, everything is in order, and

'Miss Beswick was seen by a dozen workmen . . .'

the neighbours go terror-stricken home, fully convinced that they have witnessed another of Madame Beswick's supernatural pranks.

Mr Ingram's account, published in 1905, ends there. But the Birchen Bower ghost has continued haunting, even surviving the final destruction of the barn and the building of a modern factory over the very place where the spirit used to walk. In March 1956, there was trouble in the transformer department of the works. Miss Beswick – dressed as always in black – was seen by a dozen workmen and, once again apparently, enjoying herself with machinery, just as she had done all those years ago when the labourer put a wood-lathe in his work room. Maybe Madame is still trying to point out where some of her treasure is concealed; maybe Ferranti's factory stands on a priceless hoard of old gold!

CHAPTER NINE

All your own ghosts

After reading the first of these books, *Haunted Houses*, many young readers – and a few older ones too – sent me letters telling me about ghosts they had seen or heard. I was delighted, of course, to get so many letters, and a couple of things, apart from the stories themselves, interested me particularly.

First of all, I was surprised at the number of people who said they believed in ghosts, or at least that they believed in supernatural 'spirits' of one kind or another. I had thought that what most people liked about ghost stories was simply that they can be very entertaining. But no – here was one correspondent after another, as young as eight and as old as forty, telling me that they truly believe ghosts exist and are sometimes seen by quite ordinary people.

The second thing that fascinated me was how many of those who wrote to me described encounters they themselves had had with ghosts. Nor were the accounts spiced with dramatic touches such as authors of fictional ghost stories use, but were straightforward, honest-to-goodness descriptions. Of course, there could be all kinds of natural (instead of supernatural) explanations for what many of them had experienced, and I suppose a few might have invented their tales as jokes. But none of this matters; what does matter is that, on the whole, these letters told of events which their authors sincerely believed to have been caused by ghosts.

I thought that many readers of this present book might be as interested as I was in a few of the accounts sent to me, and so I include them here. In each case I have quoted all or part of the correspondent's own words; but I have not used their full names. I have used only Christian names, or, when even then they might be too easily identified, I have given them fictional names. I have done this to protect the kind people who told me of their personal experiences from prying questions foisted on them by the morbidly curious, as well as from the weak jokes which malicious sceptics make at the expense of people who have more open minds than theirs about unusual phenomena.

Let me start with Barrie, whom I judged to be a teenager, and who sent me a vivid report of a typical haunting after a tragic death.

'I have seen a ghost,' Barrie wrote. 'It all took place about three years ago when I visited my cousins. It was a bright Sunday afternoon and we decided to go for a walk to the local beauty spot called Colley Hill. There were quite a few people up there, so we decided to go again that night. Seven-thirty came around, darkness fell and off we set. We strolled casually up to the spot where we were earlier on. There is a bench about twenty-five or thirty feet from the rim of the hill, and we looked at the view below. There were no clouds in the sky or mist anywhere, a perfectly clear night.

'But suddenly the three of us stood up at the same time and pointed in the same direction. Moving slowly across the rim of the hill floated a misty shape, about five feet in height. We stood and watched it come closer to us; but as it came nearer it increased its speed quite rapidly, and headed for a chalk pit close by. It then zoomed along towards the pit and we simply ran as fast as we could.

'I learned some years later that a small boy had fallen from the top of the pit and was killed. We have been back since but we did not see the ghost again.'

From Manchester someone I shall call Miss Emery wrote to tell me of an incident she knew of, which again resembles a great many stories associated with ghostly activity.

'In our old house in Wythenshawe there is said to be a ghost of a lady who lived there previously. Her name was Mrs Pecose, a Russian lady, I think. People say that she gassed herself, for what reason, no one knows. But in the dead of night, my family and I have heard noises in our living-room, as if someone were pacing up and down, and then the noises would stop for a while. After a few minutes we could hear footsteps coming up the stairs, but when my mother went to see who it might be, there was never anyone there. Although my family and I have never seen her, we are sure it is Mrs Pecose who haunts the house.'

Wythenshawe, which is a very large housing estate built just before and just after the Second World

War, seems to have more than one ghost troubling it. Only a few days before Miss Emery's letter reached me, fourteen-year-old Paul sent me an account of a ghost that haunted the house where his family used to live on the estate.

'The piece of land on which the houses were built used to be a farm and the site our house stood on was where the farm house used to be.

'Well, the council wanted the site for houses and the married couple [who lived in the farm house] would not sell. But then the corporation commandeered the land so the married pair were chucked out.

'The woman cursed the house and all the property, saying all the husbands of the women who lived on the land would die.

'When Mother moved in I was not born and her only child was a daughter (my thirty-year-old sister, Mary). That night my mum and sister heard a thump on the stairs of a ball and toys (at the time there was no carpet on the stairs).

'Mother had to make a trip to the chiropodist and when she showed the assistant her appointment-card the woman said, "This is my old address!"

'Mum asked her if she had a son who used to play on the stairs. The assistant said, "Yes, I had a three-year-old son but he was knocked down and killed by a road sweeping machine." Mum told the woman, to her amazement, that the boy still played on the stairs! And as far as I know he still does. Probably a poltergeist.

'As for myself, all the years in that house I was

always aware at night of an intense cold in the bedroom and I never went upstairs on my own. And no one stayed in the house more than a couple of years except us.'

Ethereal nuns figure in many ghost stories. Dennis, who must be about twelve or thirteen, sent me his story involving one such spirit.

'Very close to where I live is a big place called a priory. The story goes that there was a great fire which gutted half the house. No one was there at the time except for a nun, who had been seeing a man secretly. She was burned to death, but none of the other nuns in the place helped to save her. Since then a lot of my friends have said they have seen a ghost. Myself and two other friends have also seen "it".

'What I saw was a person dressed in a black dress, with white on the inside of the hood. Andrew noticed it first, saying, "Is that your mum?" I looked, and she seemed to be staring just above us as if looking for someone [Dennis and his pals were up a tree at this time]. We scrambled down but she seemed to have gone through a door into [what used to be] the living-room. We went there, but no one was inside.

'Andrew said, "She's gone!" But then I realized there was no other exit to the room, as the doors had been blocked up. We looked at each other, then just ran. We haven't been near that room since!'

Not all the stories sent to me were about events in which the person writing to me had been involved. Often they were about legends told in the area where the person lived. Catherine sent me the one that follows, a well-known haunting by a black abbot who

'I saw a person dressed in a black dress . . .'

wanders through part of Cheltenham where Catherine lives.

'On certain nights the ghost walks up St Mary's church tower and down again, goes through the wall of the church and into the Priory, where a family live. It goes through the house and the lady who lives there says she has seen it. Then it walks through the huge garden and into another cottage. The lady who lives there told me all about this when I went to buy some apples for her last summer. She also says she has seen it, walking silently through her house. Next it goes across the road into yet another cottage. It performs the same act as before, walking through the house. Then across the road again and into the house of one of Cheltenham's MPs. I don't know if he has seen it! Then it goes back into the church.'

More puzzling and much more frightening than the abbot are the sounds which disturbed seventeen-year-old Rosemary at her London home.

'One night about five or six years ago my family and I had gone to bed. My sister and I were sleeping in the living-room because our bedroom, which was at the far end of our flat, was being decorated. We slept in single beds which were about a foot away from each other. My sister went off like a light, but even though I was tired I just could not get to sleep. Suddenly I heard footsteps. Then it was as though the "thing" leapt from the middle of the room to the side of my bed. I looked around the room but I could not see anything. Then something whispered "Meloney". I called out to my dad. The footsteps went out of the living-room and stopped.

'My dad came in and told me not to be silly and to go to sleep. When he went back to bed and all the lights were out once more, my sister and I could hear the footsteps once more. I think that it was a man, judging from the way the "thing" said "Meloney".

'Some time ago when we were back in our bedroom, I was just going to sleep when I heard a tapping on the wall. It came from the living-room. We had a dog at the time, and while the tapping was going on the dog was making strange noises and crying. I called out to see if my dad or my brother was in the room. But no one called back. I told my sister, who was awake by now, but as I was telling her the noises stopped! I asked my dad and brother about it next morning but they said it was not them as they had gone to bed. So I do not know what it was. But I know one thing: it will happen again.'

A particularly interesting kind of ghost story I have come across now and again is one in which a dying person's ghost is seen, just at the moment of death, by someone else. It is usually a friend or relative to whom the ghost appears, even though they may be many miles away from the place where the death happens, and may know nothing at all about it. A boy called Keith sent me a very good account of this kind.

'In my grandfather's school there was a boy named Ferdinand who was one of my grandfather's greatest pals while he was at school. Being a practical joker Ferdinand often used to play pranks like jumping out on people to startle them.

'Many years later my grandfather heard about a

reunion of the old boys of the school. He packed his bags in order to spend a few nights at the school. And when he got there his first question was, "Where is Father Ferdinand?" – for Ferdinand had become a friar. The answer was "Oh, haven't you been told? He took ill a few weeks ago and because of the reunion he was taken to a place in Scotland four hundred miles away in case the excitement was too much for him."

'The day passed and my grandfather went to bed early in order to get a good night's sleep. He woke up in the early hours to find he was sweating and felt boiling hot. So he went downstairs to the big oak door that led into the garden. But being old the door had many bolts and locks on it; because of this he decided to go through the vestry so as not to wake anyone else who was sleeping.

'While walking through the vestry someone came out from one of the arches and joined him. It was not until the person spoke that my grandfather realized that the person was Ferdinand.

'When out in the garden Father Ferdinand asked my grandfather what he had done with himself since they had last met. So my grandfather launched into his tale and while he was telling it he was gazing round the garden.

'The minutes passed away and just as the church clock struck four my grandfather turned to say that that was all he could remember. To his amazement no one was there.

'Thinking that Father Ferdinand was going to play one of his practical jokes, he started for the vestry, saying quite loudly, "I'm going in now. I'll leave the door open if you want to follow me in." He then said good night and went indoors.

'Early next morning my grandfather came downstairs to find only one man eating. So he joined him and asked if Father Ferdinand had had breakfast yet. The man gave him a puzzled look and said, "I thought you knew that . . ." My grandfather cut him short and said, "If you were going to say that Father Ferdinand is in Scotland, you're mistaken. I was talking to him in the garden last night." Hearing this, the man got up and left the room without a single word.

'A few minutes later he came back and asked my grandfather to go with him. He led my grandfather to the notice board, which said, much to his amazement and disappointment, "Let us offer our prayers for the repose of the soul of Father Ferdinand, who died at four o'clock this morning."

'Seeing this, my grandfather believed that he had seen a ghost and has done ever since.'

These, then, are some of the stories that have been sent to me over the last year. I want to give my thanks to everyone who wrote to me, and to thank especially those who have allowed me to quote their letters here.

If you have enjoyed this Piccolo book, you may like to choose your next book from the titles listed on the following pages

Other Ghost Stories by Aidan Chambers are also available in Piccolo

Haunted Houses
line drawings 128pp 20p

Great British Ghosts
line drawings 128pp 25p

Great Ghosts of the World
line drawings 128pp 25p

Sorche Nic Leodhas
Scottish Ghosts
192pp 30p
Twenty tales from the Highlands of Scotland, many of them new to print, all of them satisfactorily weird and spine-chillingly vivid.

Piccolo Fiction

Rudyard Kipling

The Jungle Book, and *The Second Jungle Book*, first published in 1894 and 1895, are not only fables illustrating profound truths, but also thrilling and exciting stories.

Puck of Pook's Hill and *Rewards and Fairies*, in which Kipling brings vividly to life the most exciting moments in English history, as Puck confronts the two children with some very interesting people . . .

All at 50p

Just So Stories tells you fascinating things like How the Camel got his Hump, and How the Leopard got his Spots. 40p

Piccolo Non-Fiction